# DIVERSE LONDON

# DIVERSE LONDON

Twenty Walks Exploring London's Wonderfully Varied Communities

Written & illustrated by
DAVID FATHERS

CONWAY
LONDON • OXFORD • NEW YORK • NEW DELHI • SYDNEY

**Who's who**

*Opposite page; clockwise from the top left corner.*

Isaac Rosenberg
Paul Robeson
Sadiq Khan
Mary Seacole
William Butler Yeats
Benjamin Disraeli
Princess Sophia Duleep Singh
Rudolph Rocker
The Kinder Transport Memorial
V K Krishna Menon
Sir Trevor McDonald
Samuel Coleridge-Taylor
Dr Philip Lamb
Sir John Houblon
Sir Learie Constantine
Noor Inayat Khan
Nathan Mayer Rothschild
Ignatius Sancho

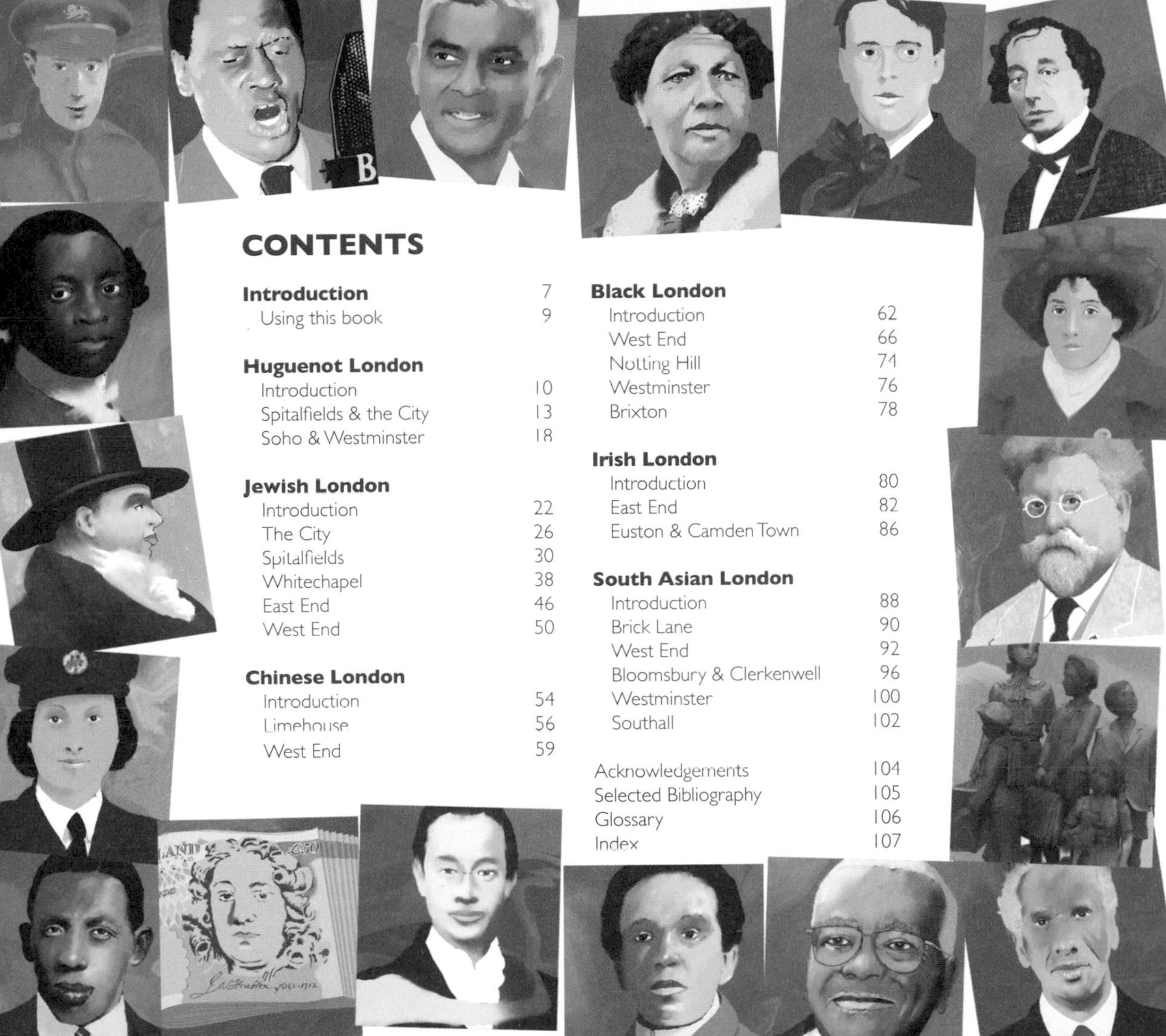

# CONTENTS

*'And the more I learn of the different places of London life, the surer and deeper is my belief in humanity, love and beauty. Why should people be separated by terms of race or nation'*

**Chiang Yee**
*The Silent Traveller in London*
*1938*

*Opposite page: the Brick Lane Jamme Masjid Mosque.*

# INTRODUCTION

Some years ago, as I was walking along Brick Lane, just to the east of the City of London, I noticed a fine, large, brick-built Georgian edifice. A sundial was set into the south facing gable with the Latin inscription '*Umbra Sumus*' ('we are but shadows') just above it. As I got closer towards the construction, I was struck by a very contemporary stainless steel minaret adjacent to it, on the corner with Fournier Street. This was the Brick Lane Mosque. Obviously, the building had not always been designated as such. In fact, this gathering place was created nearly 280 years ago, first serving as a Protestant Huguenot church, then a Wesleyan chapel, before becoming an Orthodox Jewish synagogue in 1897 and finally being converted to a mosque nearly 80 years later. With each wave of newly arrived settlers to the area, this building has not only served their spiritual needs but has also acted as a community centre, meeting place and a school.

## Spitalfields and Whitechapel

For nearly three hundred years the districts of Spitalfields and Whitechapel attracted incomers. Close to the docks, where many immigrants arrived, they offered employment in the textile and related industries, employing skills that some migrants brought with them or that could be quickly learned. They also offered cheap accommodation. While this book isn't exclusively devoted to these two areas, they have come to represent the story of Diverse London in so many ways.

## Londinium and the new arrivals

London has always been a hybrid city. From the time the Romans arrived and established Londinium, many of the soldiers, administrators and traders were not native Romans but people from countries adjacent to the Mediterranean Sea. By the eleventh century, London was a trading hub, inhabited by Danes, Saxons, Franks, Jutes, Angles and Gauls.

The numerous migrants who have arrived in London over the past two thousand years have often been driven from their homelands by oppression or starvation. In the twentieth century they have been invited here to assist in rebuilding a war-torn country and to staff the newly nationalised industries and the National Health Service. And more recently, until the Brexit referendum, EU citizens were permitted to live and work in the UK.

Life has not always been easy for these new arrivals; many have faced trauma, hostility from certain members of the British-born population, and the trials of learning a new language and culture. However, in return for opportunities and a home, these settlers have introduced fresh, new ideas and practices in so many areas of life, industry, banking, politics, reform, education, literature, cookery, entertainment and the arts. I have developed this guidebook and its curated walks to reveal some of the stories each group has encountered as they've settled in the capital.

# USING THIS BOOK

This book features 20 walks of distances varying from 1.0km to 8.3km, shown just below each chapter title. Each route could easily be walked in a reverse sequence, if desired. The walks featured in this book cover a total of 70km (or 43 miles).

I have, where possible, opted for quieter paths, away from busy main roads. Though they may not be the shortest route, they often prove to be more interesting.

The route is indicted with a red dotted line. Occasionally a path or street may be closed due to building or engineering work. In these circumstances there are usually alternative routes signposted by the contractor.

All nearby Underground, Overground and railway stations are clearly marked on the maps throughout the book.

## Symbols

# HUGUENOT LONDON

## Persecution and banishment

Around the mid-sixteenth century a wave of revolt against the domination of the Roman Catholic Church swept across Europe. In France, the dissenters were initially known as Calvinists – followers of the Lutheran theologian John Calvin – but they soon became better known as Huguenots. Originally a term of abuse targeted at them, members soon adopted the name to differentiate themselves from other branches of Protestantism. The term Huguenot may have been an amalgamation of a sixteenth-century Swiss politician named Besançon Hugues and the Dutch word *huisgenoten* (housemates). Others believed that the term came from the tenth-century king of the Franks, Hugues Capet.

The Huguenots believed in a predestination, chosen or elected by God; some were destined to salvation while others were not. But, unlike the Quakers, it would not set them apart from their Anglican Protestant neighbours. As persecution of the Huguenots increased, some families fled France to other, safer havens across Europe, including the Protestant domain of England under the rule of Elizabeth I.

During the last four decades of the sixteenth century, the Huguenots began to resist oppression and anti-Catholic riots broke out across France. These became known as the French Wars of Religion.

Matters really came to a head on the eve of the feast of St Bartholomew, on 23 August 1572. Many prominent and wealthy Huguenots gathered for the wedding of Charles IX's sister, Margo, to Protestant King Henry III of Navarre. Charles' mother, Catherine de' Medici, orchestrated the assassination of a leading Huguenot, Admiral Coligny. Following his murder, thousands of Huguenots in Paris rose up in defence. Royalist soldiers went on the offensive and assassinated the assembled Huguenot leaders, their wives and children. The killing spree spread to cities well beyond Paris. It is believed that around 10,000 Huguenots were massacred over several days.

**Edict of Nantes** In 1598, King Henry III of Navarre ascended the French throne, as Henry IV, though only after converting to Catholicism. With some fickleness he declared 'the spirit of Paris is worth a Mass'.

In the same year he issued the Edict of Nantes, which gave Protestants, including Huguenots, freedom to worship without persecution. However, for Huguenots this protection was really only paper-thin. They were still banned from trade guilds in many cities and the King's dragoons were billeted in some Huguenot's houses, in an attempt to harass them into converting to Catholicism. So faced with this intimidation, thousands more fled abroad.

*Below: the aftermath of the St Bartholemew's Day massacre. Right: the destinations and number of Huguenot refugees that left France during the reign of Louis XIV (1643-1715).*

**Revocation** Louis XIV ascended the French throne in 1643. Huguenots were still under increasing pressure to convert to Catholicism or flee the country. In 1685, Louis issued the Edict of Fontainebleau, which banned all Protestant services and prohibited Huguenots from emigrating, as France was now beginning to suffer from a shortage of talent and skills. Around 200,000 Huguenots had already fled to the Netherlands, South Africa, North America, Ireland and England. Those who managed to escaped prior to the Revocation often managed to get money and possessions out of the country, too. In 1681, the English king, Charles II, a cousin of Louis XIV, who had himself been banished from his homeland during the Civil War, took pity on the French Huguenots and began a campaign to raise funds to assist the newly arrived refugees.

**A place to worship** The Huguenots needed somewhere to practice their religion in their newly adopted country, without fear of reprisal or attack. Earlier in 1550, under the reign of Edward VI, a French Protestant church was established on Threadneedle Street, within the City, as a church for 'strangers' (immigrants). A century later it became a religious focal point for Huguenot refugees and a centre of education *(page 16)*.

Charles II assigned the French Church of the Savoy, on Savoy Hill, to the Huguenots in 1661. The Savoy Church resisted overtures from the Threadneedle Street Church to amalgamate the two, however a petition was sent to Charles II to close the Savoy Chapel and expand its sphere. Threadneedle Street had claimed it was loyal to the Crown during the Civil War. The Savoy Chapel was only able to survive by adopting a French translation of the Anglican prayer book. This was not what many Huguenots of Westminster wanted, but it was better than no church at all.

However, the Savoy Chapel was within the sphere of Westminster power and influence. This split the congregation into two camps; those in the east, who were largely merchants, weavers and sailors, and those in the west, who were military officers, tradesmen: wigmakers, clockmakers and workers of precious metals. The current Savoy Chapel was rebuilt in 1839, following a fire. It is now known as the Queen's Chapel of the Savoy.

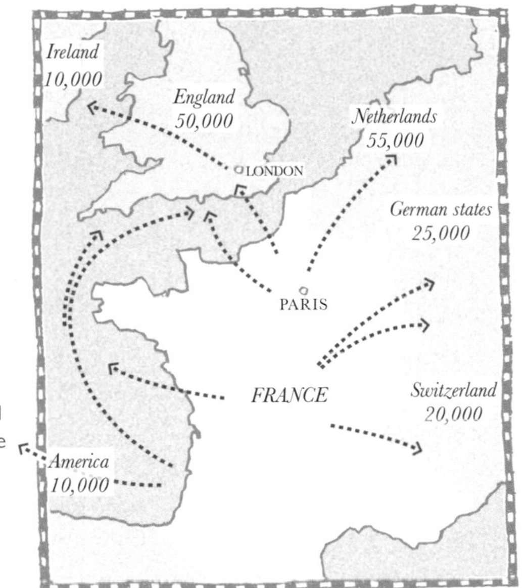


Refugees arriving in London had a choice of congregations – the conformist Savoy Chapel of Westminster or the non-conformist church in Threadneedle Street. Many of the newly arrived weavers headed to Threadneedle Street, as not only did it follow the religious beliefs for which they had left the country of their births but it also had a successful relief programme to support impoverished Huguenots.

From 1681, the Anglican Church began donating alms to the Huguenot refugees. William III also contributed £39,000 to the charity in the same year. This wasn't a totally altruistic donation, as he would need to recruit Huguenot soldiers for future military campaigns.

**Charity** Committees were formed with the aim of providing alms for struggling Huguenots; usually those just arrived from France, often with nothing more than they could carry. This aid came usually in the form of soup kitchens and hospitals. A French hospital, La Providence, opened in 1718 on Bath Street, near Old Street. It is still operating today, although it has relocated to Rochester in Kent and provides accommodation for elderly Huguenot descendants.

As the number of Huguenots increased, especially after the Revocation, so too did the number of churches in London. These were constructed in the newly formed suburbs of Soho and Spitalfields. In 1724, L'Église de l'Hôpital was built on Brick Lane. This building would later be turned into a synagogue, and after that a chapel and a mosque *(page 90)*. By 1700, the number of Huguenot chapels in London had increased to nine. Huguenots became the most dominant group of immigrants in the Spitalfields area.

**The silk weavers** Spitalfields was, by the 1680s, an area of rural land, a former artillery field and a priory, onto which debris from the 1666 Great Fire had been deposited. Speculative builders began to construct houses for those displaced by the recent fire.

The presence of English silk ribbon weavers already operating in Spitalfields encouraged many of the Huguenot silk producers from south and west France to move here, with its access to raw materials, a ready market for their wares and the area being beyond the control of the City Guilds. Between 1689 and 1716, three-fifths of all those registered at the Huguenot La Patente Church on Hanbury Street, were involved in the textile trade.

Silk weaving was usually conducted in the lofts of the new houses, where the light was better. These were invariably family-run businesses with the entire household working on various stages of production. It was soon acknowledged that the newcomers were able to produce cloth in wider bolts and of a superior quality than that created by their English counterparts, and a new type of silk industry grew in the capital. Huguenot cloth was an expensive, sophisticated commodity that required numerous layers of production, resulting in a beautiful product which became the height of fashion. Raw silk was usually imported from Italy or China by boat, into the nearby Port of London. Silk weaving, before the Industrial Revolution, was a major industry, not just in east London but also across England. It was vital to the nation's wealth, coming, as it did, at the expense of the French economy.

The Huguenots had, by sheer necessity, the will to succeed in their newly adopted country and they out-performed many of the English-born weavers. In 1692, they established Royal Lustring Company and soon acquired nearly 700 looms. These were being operated by freelance weavers within private loft-spaces in the Spitalfields and Bethnal Green area.

**Reaction and riots** Despite a certain level of support from the monarchy, the Huguenots were not universally welcome in the city. In 1661, long after the Spanish Armada, Samuel Pepys wrote in his diary *'we do naturally all love the Spanish, and hate the French'*. Five years later, both during and after the Great Fire of London, many Londoners suspected immigrants had started the conflagration. Some English workers felt their livelihoods were threatened by the arrivals from France; they worshipped at a different church, ate strange foods and even spoke a different language.

In 1675, riots broke out over the introduction of weaving machines that could do the work of several men. Weavers' homes were broken into and the engine looms destroyed. The threat of violence against the Spitalfields Huguenot weavers appeared again at the end of the seventeenth century. Occasionally riots broke out between the Irish silk weavers of Bethnal Green and French weavers over rates of pay, as one group would undercut the other. In one riot, nearly a hundred years later, the militia killed two weavers and two rioters were hung. Ironically, it was Huguenot weavers who provided new production expertise and gainful employment for the local English population. Yet, on balance, the greeting the Huguenots received could be described as hospitable. Other groups of migrants would not receive such a warm welcome.

**The decline of silk production** The Spitalfields Act of 1773 enforced a minimum wage upon the owners, who were happy to see looms stand idle rather than pay the recommended increase. In the 1790s, demand for silk had slumped and it was reported that 4,000 looms in Spitalfields were now idle. The Napoleonic Wars (1803-1815) created a greater need for silk produced in the UK, as the European supply was closed off. But following the wars, the silk trade in the UK declined again, as French silk producers re-entered the marketplace and forced prices down. The Spitalfields silk trade would continue to gradually decline throughout the nineteenth century as owners moved production away from London and alternative fabrics such as cotton became cheaper and more plentiful. By 1914, there were just 46 silk workshops in Spitalfields and Bethnal Green.

# SPITALFIELDS & THE CITY

*Total walking distance 2.7km*

This walk, through the streets just to the east of the City, takes in many former locations of prominent Huguenot weavers, several of whom would become well-known names centuries later.

**1 La Patente Church** Many migrating Huguenots opted to move to Spitalfields because of the proximity of the non-conformist French Church on Threadneedle Street. By the end of the seventeenth century, with the increased influx of Huguenots, new churches were desperately needed. One, La Patente, was initially established close to what is now the Spitalfields Market, before moving to Hanbury Street in 1719 (it is now the Hanbury Community Centre, see *page 13*). By the early part of the eighteenth century there were nine Huguenot churches in Spitalfields.

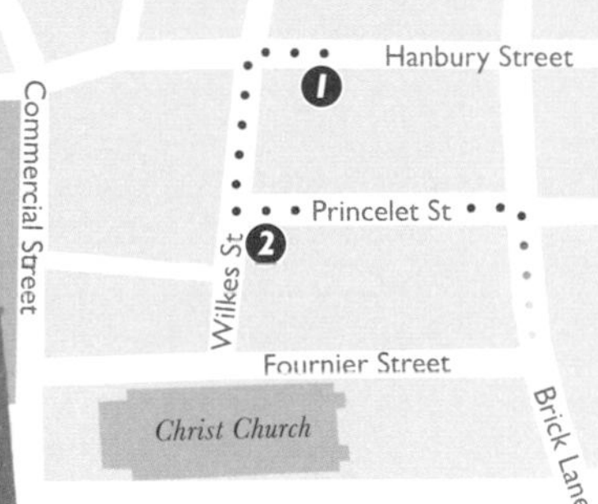


**2 Anna Maria Garthwaite** Garthwaite was a hugely influential silk pattern designer who, in 1728, moved into 2 Princelet Street (the house had only been built five years earlier). Garthwaite was English, female and the child of an Anglican minister and his wife. Regardless of this, she broke into the world of Huguenot silk weaving and was commissioned by several leading master weavers including her neighbour *(page 14)*. In her lifetime she created over a thousand bespoke silk patterns based on highly visual botanical and Rococo motifs, many of which were sold beyond the shores of England to wealthy colonialists. She died at her Princelet Street home in 1763. Today, a plaque marks the house.

**Vatican red hats** With some irony, the red birettas worn by Roman Catholic cardinals in the Vatican used to be made by Huguenot hatters in Wandsworth, south-west London.

*Clockwise from left: 2 Princelet Street, the house and workshop of Anna Maria Garthwaite; a silk weaver at his loom; a silk biretta, made by Huguenots.*

*1* **19 Princelet Street** In 1697, seven-year-old Peter Abraham Ogier fled France, along with his mother and several of his siblings, and headed to Spitalfields. Within a matter of years Peter took up an apprenticeship as a silk weaver.

In 1712, he married Esther Dubois and they went on to produce 12 children. Ogier was extremely entrepreneurial and quickly built a sizeable silk weaving company. By 1716, he become a freeman of the Weavers' Company. In the 1740s, he and his family moved into 19 Princelet Street. This would be a strictly residential abode with no looms operating from the address. The three-storey house by Samuel Worrall, master carpenter to Nicholas Hawksmoor, was built in 1718 and still stands today. It has seen numerous transformations over the centuries *(page 32)*. Peter died in 1757 and although several of the Ogier children were buried in Christ Church, it is not certain if Peter or his wife were buried here. The extended Ogier family went on to be very successful and influential both in Spitalfields and North America during the eighteenth century.

**Courtauld** Another member of the Ogier family would go on to be an even greater influential industrialist. Peter Abraham's niece Louisa Perina Ogier married Samuel Courtauld, a Huguenot goldsmith, in 1749, and produced four children. Their eldest son, George, became a Spitalfields silk weaver and later went on to create a silk yarn and cloth production factory in Essex. However, after the Napoleonic Wars, Courtauld & Co. experienced financial difficulties, at which point George decided to retire, leaving his eldest son, Samuel, to manage the company. It was through his management that the textile company expanded into an international operation. Finally, in 1990 the company was broken up and sold.

Another Samuel Courtauld, the great-nephew of the industrialist and a CEO of Courtauld's, developed a large collection of Impressionist and Post-Impressionist art. In 1932, he founded the Courtauld Institute of Art on the Strand.

**2 The House of many faiths** On the corner of Brick Lane and Fournier Street stands the Brick Lane Mosque *(page 90)*. The structure was originally a Huguenot chapel, L'Église Neuve, built in 1743. The original sundial with the inscription *Umbra Sumus* ('We are but shadows' – a reference to man's fleeting time on earth) is still in place today. The vaults were leased out to the local brewery. By the early nineteenth century it had become a Wesleyan chapel, before being transformed into a Jewish synagogue in 1897.

**3 27 Fournier Street** This fine double-fronted house was built for Pierre Bourdain, a Huguenot weaver. The head of the downpipe (upper right side) denotes the year the house was constructed, 1725.

**4 John Sabatier** In 1750, master weaver John Sabatier owned a large warehouse on Fournier Street, with a great number of looms stationed within. It is believed that he owned 50 looms across his operation, though they were not all located here. It is more likely that he commissioned outworkers. Many of his woven designs came from Anna Maria Garthwaite. Such was Sabatier's wealth and fortune that in 1745, he was able to pledge 34 members of his staff to fight for George II in the war with the Jacobites.

**5 The Lekeux Family** Peter Lekeux III was a wealthy and successful third-generation Huguenot weaver and Spitalfields landowner. In the first half of the seventeenth century, Peter Lekeux III's family had departed France and relocated in Canterbury. In 1755, he commissioned two yellow brick three-storey houses to be built at 1 and 3 Fournier Street (he chose to live at the latter). Both are still standing today. Peter III's company was renowned for producing very lavish and expensive silks for men's garments. Anna Maria Garthwaite designed many of the silk fabrics his weavers created.

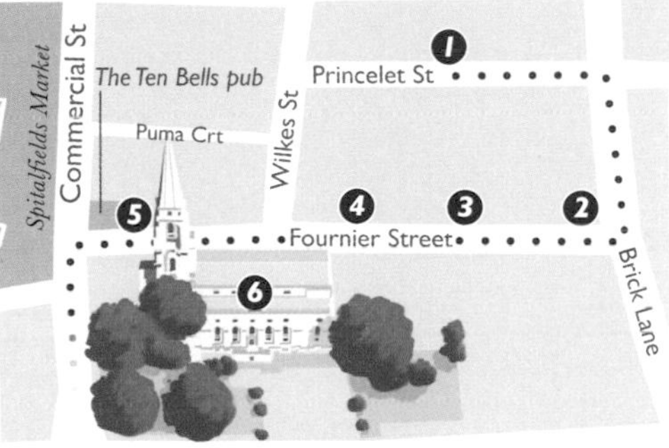


**6 Christ Church Spitalfields** By the turn of the eighteenth century, the non-conformist Huguenots had nine chapels in the Spitalfields area. This did not go unnoticed by the Church of England and in 1711 they commissioned Nicholas Hawksmoor, a protégé of Sir Christopher Wren, to design a church for the new parish. It's very possible that the brief was to create a structure that

*Clockwise from left: the logo for Courtaulds plc, (formerly Courtauld & Co.); the sundial on the former Huguenot chapel (now the Brick Lane Mosque) on Fournier Street; the western elevation of Christ Church Spitalfields; house numbers 1 and 3 Fournier Street, once home of the Lekeux family; a wooden spool hanging outside 37 Fournier Street; a downpipe head at 27 Fournier Street.*

would dominate the neighbourhood. Standing at 62 metres high, it certainly did then and still does today. The Baroque church was consecrated in 1729.

Despite being an Anglican church, many wealthy Huguenots were buried here, as their own churchyards simply did not have sufficient space for interments. Members of the Ogier and the Courtauld families are buried within the grounds of Christ Church.

Within Christ Church, close to the altar, is a statue of Sir Robert Ladbroke, dated 1794. Ladbroke was a city merchant banker, a prominent member of the Spitalfields Huguenot society and, from 1754, a Member of Parliament.

**Wooden spools** Outside several eighteenth-century houses in Spitalfields hang large wooden spools *(right)*. These were placed there in 1985 to commemorate the tercentenary of the Revocation of the Edict of Nantes. There is example an of a wooden spool hanging at number 37 Fournier Street.

*Walking these pages 0.3km*

**1 The Bell Lane Workhouse** In 1728, a workhouse was established on Bell Lane. The majority of its 80 workers, including children, were tasked with creating silk thread from the imported raw material silkworm fibre. The finished thread was then sold to local weavers.

**2 56–58 Artillery Lane** This surviving Georgian shop front *(above)* was, in 1757, owned by Nicholas Jourdain and Francis Rybot, both weavers, who also sold their own silk in the shop below the looms. Jourdain was also a director of the French hospital, La Providence.

**3 The Cock** In the seventeenth century The Cock public house, in Widegate Street (formerly Whitegate Alley) became a focal point of unrest against the Huguenot weavers. Many English silk weavers met here and planned to attack their French counterparts. In August 1683, when word of a potential riot reached Charles II, he stationed numerous garrisons on the outskirts of Spitalfields to deter any attacks. This seemed to have had a sobering effect on the rioters, as no incidents were reported. However, the bitterness would not evaporate and later flared up. The pub is no longer standing.

**4 L'Église de L'Artillerie** (the Artillery Church). This was once the site of a Huguenot chapel that opened in 1766. It was built on the site of a former military training ground. A hundred years later, as the Huguenot population declined in Spitalfields, it was sold and was converted into the Sandy Row Synagogue. It is now the oldest surviving Ashkenazi synagogue in London *(page 30)*.

**5 James Leman** (1688-1745) James Leman was a second generation Huguenot weaver who, unusually, was a silk fabric designer too. Having been apprenticed to his father for four years, he started designing at the age of 18. From his workshop in Steward Street he created hundreds of fabulous designs that were a combination of floral, geometric and architectural motifs, some of which included metallic threads that sparkled in candlelight. His fashionable product was very much in demand in both Europe and North America. He was accepted into the Weavers' Company and rose quickly through the ranks, despite his 'foreign' status. Ninety of his patterns are held in the V&A Museum and are the oldest surviving set of silk designs in the world.

**6 Dennis Severs' House** An American-born artist, Dennis Severs bought this early eighteenth-century house at 18 Folgate Street in 1979. He then restored the house, room by room, to tell the story of a wealthy Huguenot silk weaving family, the Jervis', who lived here from 1724 until the late nineteenth century. The house, which is open to the public, is only illuminated by candle and gas lights. Each room appears, with its unmade beds and half eaten meals, as if the owners have just vanished before your arrival. The house is open to the public on certain days *(see www.dennisseversshouse.co.uk)*.

Folgate
Bishopsgate
*Liverpool St Station*
7
Threadneedle Street
Finch Lane
Bank of England
Cornhill
Princess St
8
9
Change Alley
*Bank Underground*
Lombard St
Mansion House St

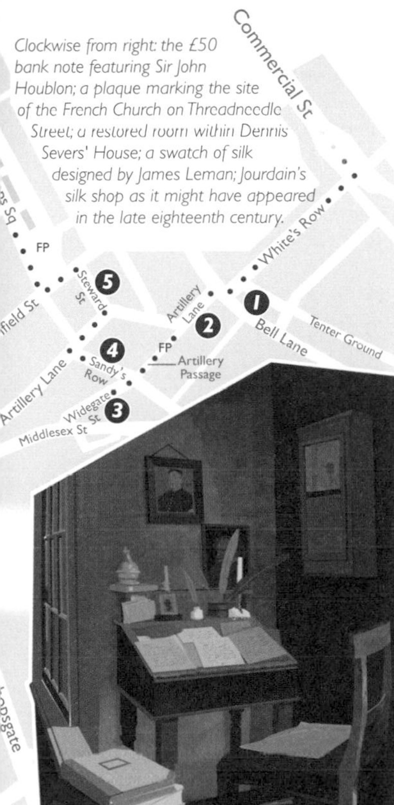


*Clockwise from right: the £50 bank note featuring Sir John Houblon; a plaque marking the site of the French Church on Threadneedle Street; a restored room within Dennis Severs' House; a swatch of silk designed by James Leman; Jourdain's silk shop as it might have appeared in the late eighteenth century.*

**7 The French Church** Nicolas des Gallars, a close associate of the French Protestant John Calvin, founded this French Church at 53 Threadneedle Street in 1550. Understandably, the church was a magnet for the escaping Huguenots in the following century and became the largest French congregation in England. Following its destruction in the Great Fire, the church was very quickly rebuilt in 1669, with Huguenot funds. Many of the Threadneedle Street Huguenot congregation lived in nearby newly developing Spitalfields. In the nineteenth century the congregation relocated to St Martin's-Le-Grand and finally, in 1888, to Soho Square.

**8 John Houblon** The Houblon family had escaped from Lille long before the anti-Protestant repressions began and were able to move much of their wealth out of the country. Sir John Houblon, a third generation Huguenot, became the first governor of the Bank of England in 1694. The bank had been established to revolutionise finances in England following a prolonged war with the French. Of the original £1.2 million deposited in the Bank of England, around 10 per cent came from Huguenot pockets. The Houblon's house, close to Threadneedle Street, was later acquired by the bank, as it needed to enlarge its operation. Houblon also sat on the Board of the English Committee, a charity distributing funds to fellow Huguenots who had fallen upon hard times since arriving in London. In 1994, to commemorate the 300th anniversary of the Bank of England, Houblon's portrait was featured on the £50 note.

**9 Jonathan's Coffee House** In the late seventeenth century a Huguenot broker, John Castaing, began publishing a weekly newspaper, *The Course of the Exchange*, which was dedicated to listing market prices of government loans and several basic commodities such as coal and salt. Castaing was known to gather much of his information while frequenting Jonathan's Coffee House in Change Alley, the daily prices of stock being displayed upon the walls. The brokers of London and other parts of Europe soon came to rely on his publication. It would later evolve into the *Stock Exchange Official Daily List.*

SITE OF THE
13TH. CENTURY HOSPITAL
OF ST. ANTHONY, AND
OF THE FRENCH
PROTESTANT CHURCH
DEMOLISHED 1840

**Refugee** The word 'refugee' first appeared in the English language not long after the Revocation of the Edict of Nantes in 1685. The *Oxford English Dictionary* defines 'refugee' as 'a Protestant who has fled France to refuge elsewhere', though the term has since expanded to cover all people fleeing from war, disaster, political or religious oppression.

*Walking these pages 2.2km*

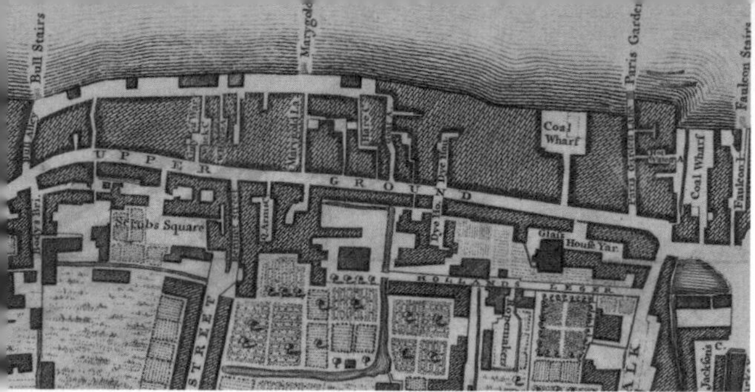


# SOHO & WESTMINSTER

*Total walking distance 3.8km*

While many of the early Huguenot refugees headed to Spitalfields, to the east of the City, with their weaving skills, those artisans of gold and silver, engraving and design moved into the newly developed district of Soho, within Westminster.

***1* Roget's Thesaurus** The creator of the *Thesaurus of English Words and Phrases*, Peter Mark Roget, was born in Broad (now Broadwick) Street, Soho, in 1779. Roget went on to study medicine in Edinburgh in 1793 and with assistance from his uncle, Samuel Romilly, he returned to London and began to make a name for himself in his chosen career (Roget was present as a doctor, at the death of his uncle in 1818).

From an early age Roget had been a fanatical list-maker and in 1805 he began to compile a classification of words arranged by meanings. Once he had retired from medicine, Roget devoted himself to preparing his thesaurus, with its 990 headings, for publication in 1852. After his death, at the age of 91, his son continued to revise and publish the thesaurus. It is still in print today.

**2 John Rocque** The map engraver John Rocque was born in 1704 into a French Huguenot family. Like many Huguenots at the time, his family had to flee France, first to Geneva and then on to London, where they arrived in 1709. After an apprenticeship, Rocque initially worked with his brother Bartholomew, a landscape gardener, producing garden plans. Rocque established his first business premises in Great Windmill Street, Soho, probably close to his parents' lodgings, before moving on to offices on Piccadilly.

Rocque is best known for the detailed and pioneering *Map of London.* He began surveying the city in 1738 on behalf of the engraver John Pine and the map was published by John Tinney in 1746. The map revealed the expanding Georgian capital and was created in 24 sheets at a scale of 26in to the mile. It measured nearly 4m wide by 2m deep and was complete with a street index. Despite Rocque only being employed to survey this map, the series would later become known as the *Rocque Map of London*.

In the same year, Rocque himself published a 16-sheet map of London that included far more countryside than the Pine and Tinney map. Both maps featured symbols to represent trees and fields and used a single grey tone for buildings – a common feature today, but at the time this was radical. Rocque would go on to recreate over 100 detail maps of London and beyond. By the 1750s he was describing himself as 'Cartographer to the Prince of Wales' (later George III). He died in 1762.

**3 Paul de Lamerie** The Huguenots were renowned as great craftsmen of gold and silverware, and one of the most outstanding was Paul de Lamerie. De Lamerie was born in 1688 in the Netherlands and within a year his Huguenot family had moved to London to seek a more secure way of life.

Because of the quality of his work, de Lamerie was invited in 1712 to become a member of the Goldsmiths Company.

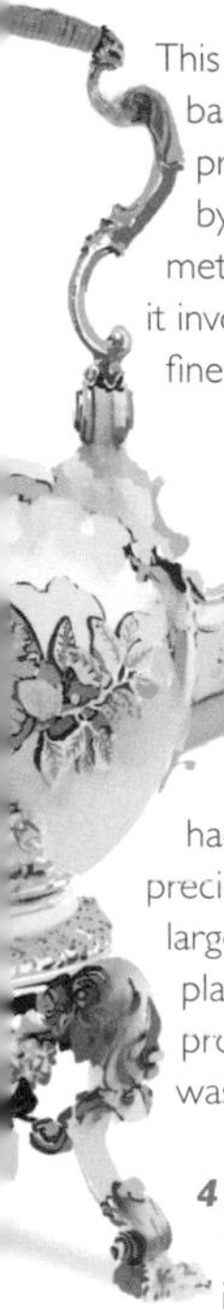

This was indeed an honour as many Huguenots were barred from joining the company. Any piece of work produced by a member of the company had to carry, by law, the hallmarks of the creator and quality of the metal. On several occasions de Lamerie failed to do this, as it involved paying duty to the company, and in 1714 he was fined £20 (equivalent to £4,000 today). Regardless of his contempt for the company he was appointed gold- and silversmith to George I in 1716. The artist and engraver William Hogarth worked on several pieces for de Lamerie's business.

As de Lamerie's fame spread, demand for his Rococo-styled gold and silver artefacts, increased. By the early eighteenth century Soho had become home to many Huguenot workers of precious metals. In 1738, de Lamerie had created a new, larger workshop and house at 40 Gerrard Street (a plaque marks the building) from where he continued to produce gold and silverware until his death in 1751. He was buried in the nearby church, St Anne's.

**4 Samuel Romilly** Samuel Romilly was born at 18 Frith Street, in 1757, son of a Huguenot jeweller. At the age of 19 he decided not to follow in his father's footsteps but instead embarked on a career as a barrister, and entered Grey's Inn to commence his training. Thirty years later, in 1806, following a successful legal career, he was offered the post of solicitor general to advise the Whig government on all matters legal, and he became MP for the constituency of Queensborough. He was knighted in the same year (between 1734 and 1832, 65 Huguenots would serve as Members of Parliament).

Romilly was an opponent of the slave trade and spoke up for the abolition campaign headed by William Wilberforce (*page 73*). In 1808, he overturned the ancient law that made theft from a person punishable by hanging. By 1814, he had abolished the gruesome act of hanging, drawing and quartering (except for treason). In 1818, Romilly died by suicide after learning about the death of his wife. In 1937, Church Street – which crosses Frith Street, his birthplace – was renamed Romilly Street in his honour.

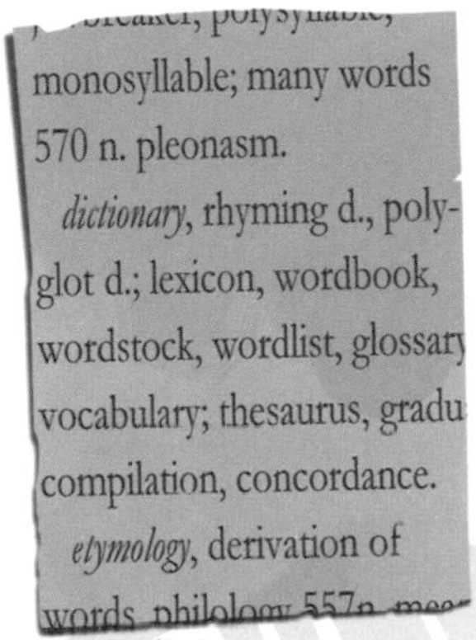
monosyllable; many words
570 n. pleonasm.
*dictionary*, rhyming d., poly-
glot d.; lexicon, wordbook,
wordstock, wordlist, glossary
vocabulary; thesaurus, gradu
compilation, concordance.
*etymology*, derivation of

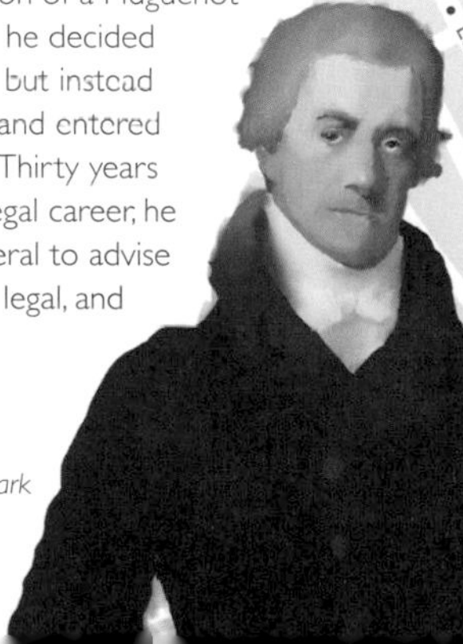

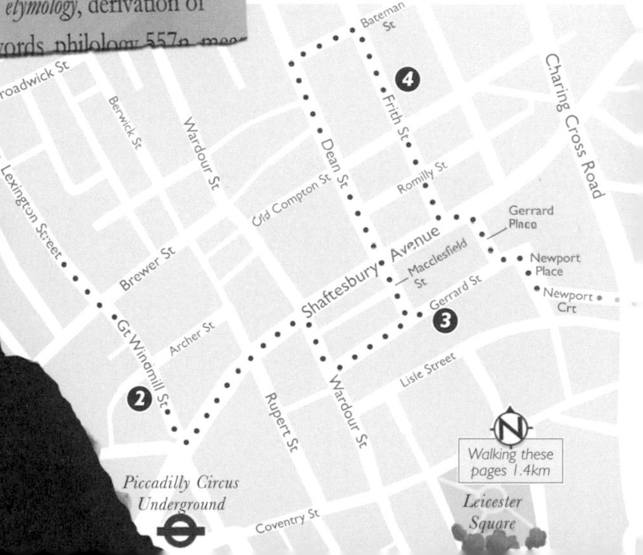


*Clockwise from top left: a detail of the map surveyed by John Rocque; a silver kettle by Paul de Lamerie; a detail from Peter Mark Roget's thesaurus; Samuel Romilly; the hallmark of Paul de Lamerie.*

***1* David Garrick** The Garrick Club and Garrick Street are both named after David Garrick, the actor, theatre manager and producer who was born to Huguenot parents in 1717 in Herefordshire. He was a third generation Huguenot, whose family name had been Anglicised from Garric to Garrick. From an early age he had shown great interest in and a talent for acting. Arriving in London in 1736, Garrick established himself as a wine merchant with his brother, but the business suffered as he was more interested in the theatre. From 1741, his fame rose rapidly, after having performed 18 roles in the space of six months.

In 1747, he became manager of the Theatre Royal, Drury Lane, and it was here that he introduced a realistic style of acting and revived interest in performing Shakespeare. He even rewrote sections, for example he gave *King Lear* a happy ending, and it drew large audiences. From 1750 until 1772 Garrick lived at 27 Southampton Street (a plaque marks the house). When he died in 1779 he was buried in Poets' Corner in Westminster Abbey.

**2 The Savoy Chapel** The church that stands on Savoy Hill, now known as the Queen's Chapel of Savoy, was entirely rebuilt following a fire in 1839. In 1661, the church had been assigned to the fleeing Huguenots by Charles II, even though a French Protestant church already existed in Threadneedle Street and was frequented by Huguenots based to the east of the City.

The division between the two churches was defined by those attending. Those who congregated at the Threadneedle Street Church were largely artisans: weavers and cloth merchants, while those of the Savoy Church were clock-makers, merchants, military officers and workers of precious metals. Each church petitioned the king to have the other closed down. The Savoy Church was able to survive but only after conforming and adopting a French translation of the book of common prayer. In return it gained royal financial patronage, and being Westminster-based made it closer to the seat of power and influence. Regardless, many newly arrived Huguenots still headed to the more traditional Protestant church in Threadneedle Street. Many members of the Savoy Church saw the adoption of English as no bad thing if they were to assimilate within their new country.

**3 Westminster Bridge** Until 1729, the only way to cross the River Thames at Westminster was to use a ferry. The nearest bridges were London Bridge to the east or Kingston Bridge miles to the west. There was clearly a need for a bridge in the heart of the expanding capital. However, objections came from the Company of Watermen and the Archbishop of Canterbury, who owned a lucrative ferry at this point in the river and did not wish for such a bridge to be built. But demand grew and, in 1741, a competition was held for bridge designs to be submitted.

Several plans were proposed, including one from Nicholas Hawksmoor, an associate

of Sir Christopher Wren, but the design tendered by Charles Labelye was selected. Labelye was born in Switzerland, in 1705, to a Huguenot family that had fled France.

Labelye's bridge was a stone-built, gentle hump-backed crossing with 15 arches. The toll-free bridge opened in 1750 and became an instant attraction. Even Canaletto visited England to paint it. However, within a hundred years the bridge began suffering the effects of strong tidal flows once the old London Bridge was removed, and it too had to be replaced in 1862.

**4 The Speaker's State Coach** Daniel Marot was a Baroque architect and furniture, interior and garden designer of great repute, especially within the court of William III. Marot, part of a Huguenot artisan family, was born in Paris, in 1661. Not long after the Revocation of the Edict of Nantes in 1684, his family fled to the Netherlands. Marot is believed to have arrived in England along with Prince William of Orange's entourage in 1688 and was responsible for, among many things, the design of the Great Fountain Garden at Hampton Court, then William III's primary residence.

In 1698, Marot was commissioned to design the State Coach for William III. His creation was a fabulously gilded Baroque structure on wheels. Following the monarch's sudden death in 1702, Queen Anne presented the carriage to the Speaker of the House of Commons. The coach is primarily used to transport the Speaker from Parliament to Westminster Abbey on the coronation of British monarchs – a journey of 350m! It was last used for the wedding of Prince Charles to Lady Diana Spencer in 1981 *(the carriage is now displayed at Arlington Court, Barnstaple, Devon).*

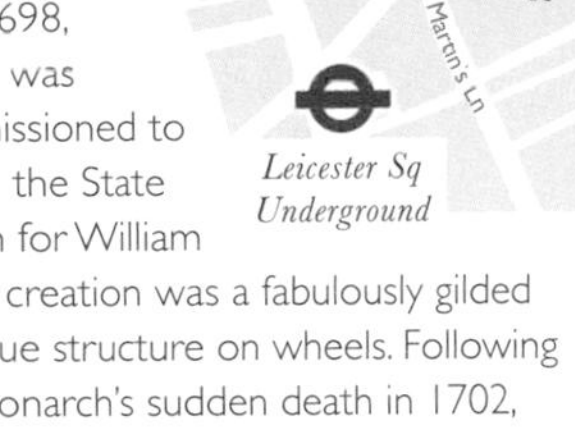


**5 Louis-Francois Roubiliac** Roubiliac was born in 1702, to Lyon silk merchants. At the age of 28, he arrived in London and first made his name as a sculptor, with a full-length seated statue of Handel posed in a relaxed style. Roubiliac became one of the greatest marble sculptors to reside in England, and fashioned statues and busts of many well-known figures including Handel and the Duke of Argyll, which can be found in Westminster Abbey* *(Westminster Abbey charges an admission fee).* He was commissioned by several fellow Huguenots, including the actor David Garrick, who appointed him to create the now famous bust of Shakespeare, for which Garrick may well have posed.

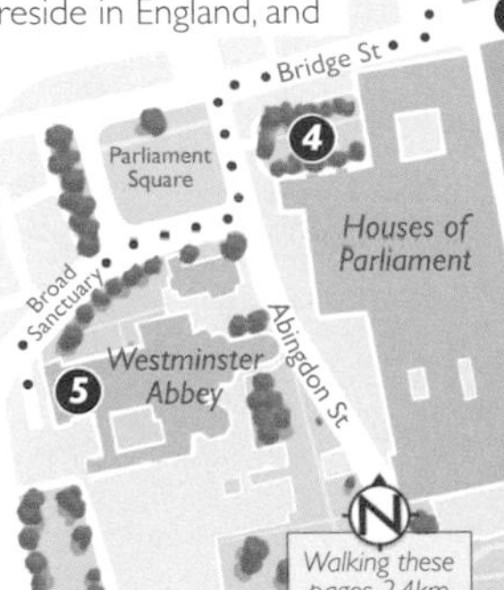


*Clockwise from top left: the rebuilt Savoy Chapel; a bust of William Shakespeare by Roubiliac (David Garrick may have been the model); the old Westminster Bridge; the Speaker's State Coach.*

# JEWISH LONDON

When William I seized the English crown in 1066, it came at a price; the invading army needed maintaining and new fortifications constructing. After all, the invading Norman army was not seen as a liberating force. Four years after the invasion, William invited Jewish people with skills in finance and commerce, from Rouen, northern France, to assist with the funding of his campaign. Jewish people across northern Europe at this time were banned from most jobs and membership of trade guilds, however they were allowed to practise medicine and usury at a time when Christians were prohibited from lending money with interest.

Members of the new Jewish community were not forced to live together but they chose to do so, to enable communal worship and procure kosher food. It is estimated that by 1100, there were about 1,000 Jewish people living in the City, around a street now known as Old Jewry. And thanks to an education system built around the synagogue, nearly all of them – men, women and children – were literate and numerate, unlike most of their English-born neighbours.

**The Backlash** While the English monarchs were happy with the usury arrangements, many English subjects were less welcoming to the Jewish community. After all, some were in debt to them. On 3 September 1189, Richard I was crowned king at Westminster Abbey. It had been decreed that Jewish people would be barred from the service, but this news never reached those wealthy Jews, who came to pay homage to the new monarch. They were attacked by members of the royal entourage and thrown out of the Abbey. Bystanders then set upon these now bloodied 'interlopers', killing several of them. Word then spread across London that all Jewish people were to be killed. In the City, several Jewish houses were burned down and some who tried to flee were attacked. It is believed that up to 30 were killed that day.

A new royal writ was issued to protect the Jewish community, since the king needed their money for his Crusades. The writ was poorly enforced and across England hundreds of them were killed, culminating in a massacre in York. The Jewish community had sought refuge in a fortified tower, but rather than accept a Christian baptism or murder at the hand of the mob, they collectively died by suicide.

It was believed that if your Jewish moneylender died so your debt vanished too. Richard, upon his return from the Crusades, decreed that this would no longer be the case, and the debt was still owed to the lender's family. In return for this guarantee, the king extracted a tax upon each transaction. The Jewish lenders were constantly viewed as a source of revenue for the monarch.

In 1199, an assassin killed Richard, and the crown fell to his younger brother, John. King John proved to be an unpopular monarch. He lost most of his French lands and therefore the rights to raise taxes there, so the burden of taxation fell upon his English subjects, the barons and the church. Like previous English monarchs, John kept the Jewish lenders close by, as he needed their services. When the disgruntled barons rose up against the king in 1215, they entered the City and attacked known royalist and Jewish people.

A settlement between the barons and the king was finally sought when the Magna Carta was signed in 1215. It included a clause which stated that once a Jewish moneylender had died, only the capital was repayable to the monarch.

Resentment of Jewish lenders and their practice of usury, often at high interest rates, swelled within the City. Matters came to a head in 1263, when an argument erupted between a Christian and a Jew outside St Mary Colechurch over the subject of interest. The Christian was attacked, and a riot followed. The area of Old Jewry, which had become home to many Jewish people, was ransacked and around 500 of them were killed.

In 1275, Edward I banned the Jewish lenders from practising usury, so they could no longer make a living. Many resorted to 'clipping the coin' – snipping off small parts of existing coins to create new ones. Three years later, over 600 Jewish people were rounded up for this crime and sent to the Tower of London, where 293, many innocent, were hung.

Finally, having been deprived of work, the Jewish community, now around 6,000 in number, were banished from England in 1290, by royal decree. Their debts and property were passed to the crown. Those who did remained converted to Christianity, though many covertly practised their beliefs. Some Jewish doctors were allowed to remain, as their skills were superior to their Christian counterparts. The edict was short-sighted, from an economical point of view, as Edward I was now unable to raise loans to fund his wars.

**The Return** In 1655, Rabbi Menasseh ben Israel petitioned the Lord Protector, Oliver Cromwell, from Amsterdam for the return of Jewish people to England. England was one of the few parts of the known world where they were not present. Upon being allowed to return, ben Israel believed that the process of Messianic Deliverance could commence. More pragmatically, England had just suffered a civil war and was in need of financial assistance.

Parliamentarians, lawyers and clergy discussed the petition, but never came to a conclusion. So, Cromwell quietly allowed the Jewish people to return. The first to arrive were the Sephardic Jews from Amsterdam, Spain and Portugal. The returnees began living in Old Jewry and Houndsditch, with the first synagogue being built nearby on Creechurch Lane with a new Sephardi cemetery established in 1657, out of town in Mile End.

**The Restoration** When Charles II returned to the throne in 1660, he enshrined protection of Jewish people into law. While exiled in the Netherlands they had assisted him financially and he was keen to offer them help upon his restoration.

However, it wasn't long before City of London authorities were petitioning the king to have the new arrivals expelled again, on the grounds that they were trading at much greater volumes and out-trading the established merchants. However, the monarch chose to ignore the petty pleas of the merchants.

Three years after the Great Fire, some Ashkenazi Jews began to arrive from eastern and central Europe. In 1690, the first Ashkenazi synagogue was established in Dukes Place. Within 30 years it had to be expanded to accommodate rising numbers of Ashkenazi Jewish arrivals.

The Ashkenazi's were seen as the 'poor Jews'; they were often street traders and peddlers, without support. Many of the Sephardi Jews of the East End resented them, irrationally fearing that they would take their jobs.

At the beginning of the eighteenth century around 1,000 Jewish people were living in London. However, this figure rose to around 20,000 within a century. The continued persecution of Jewish communities in Eastern Europe and on the Iberian Peninsula increased the rate of immigration into England. They were free under English law to live wherever they pleased, although could not hold office under the Crown or civic government (a degree of anti-Semitism was enshrined in the law).

In 1753, an Act of Parliament was proposed by a Sephardi group to give Jewish people, who had lived in Great Britain or Ireland for more than three years, naturalisation upon application. The 'Jew Act', as some referred to it, was unpopular with many MPs and with an election looming, the Act was quickly withdrawn by the end of the year.

**The Board of Deputies** At the coronation of George I in 1760, the Sephardi's offered gifts to the new king. This was much to the annoyance of the Ashkenazi's. A meeting was arranged between the two groups and a settlement

*Above: the Velho Cemetery, the oldest Jewish Cemetery in the UK, opened in 1657 on Mile End Rd.*

agreed to present a united Jewish front in England. It would become known as the Board of Deputies of British Jews.

**In Public Office** Since Henry VIII declared himself head of the Church of England in 1531, no state functions could be carried out by non-members, i.e. Roman Catholics, Jews or non-conformists. Jewish people could not be barristers, be educated at Cambridge or Oxford, nor sit in Parliament. Jewish emancipation would come in stages, piece by piece.

In 1830, the City of London decreed that anyone could now become a freeman and thus join a livery company. Five years later, Sir David Salomons, a founder of the Westminster Bank, was elected Sheriff of London. However, as he had to take a Christian oath, he was unable to take his position. In 1845, Salomons became the first Jewish mayor of the City of London, as by now all official positions were opened to the Jewish people within the City. He would later go on to become MP for Greenwich but again his religion meant he was unable to be sworn in. Salomons was unable to sit in the House of Commons until 1859, following a change in legislation. In 1833, Francis Goldsmid became the first Jew to be called to the Bar and in 1858 he joined the Queen's Counsel. The banker Nathan Mayer de Rothschild became the first Jewish peer of the realm, in 1885.

**The Reformers** The leaders of East End synagogues refused the building of new synagogues in the West End. This meant many Jewish families with West End houses had to walk a round trip of some 8 miles or so to attend service on the Sabbath. The old synagogues feared losing their congregation and the financial support they gave. In 1840, a Jewish group living in Bloomsbury began a reform movement and brought a proposal

to hold services in English. The Chief Rabbi responded with a *herem* (excommunication) of this group of 'rebels'. But the reformers went ahead and built a synagogue in Burton Street, WC1. This was not a religious schism but simply a desire to live a better life, away from the East End. Eventually, the synagogues, such as Bevis Marks, had to concede and open new synagogues in the West End. The Ashkenazi Great Synagogue followed suit by building a new place of worship in Great Portland Street.

**The Pogroms** On 13 March 1881, Tsar Alexander II of Russia was assassinated in St Petersburg. Many Russians blamed Jewish people for the assassination even though only one of the conspirators was Jewish. Regardless, Alexander III and his government introduced the May Laws in 1882. These laws prohibited them from purchasing property and conducting business on Sundays, and those living in the countryside were forced to move into the cities. This new instability and the pogroms forced millions of Jewish people to flee Russia and Poland. About 150,000 people arrived in Britain, as there were no immigration restrictions. A further 2 million would head to America.

Many of the refugees arrived on insanitary ships at Tilbury Docks, penniless and with only the clothes they were wearing. Numerous had been robbed or overcharged en route to Britain. On arrival, most headed straight to the East End, having heard that a large Jewish community already existed there.

The way of life for many settled British Jews living in the East End was about to be upturned. They feared that the sudden influx, visible by their clothes, would increase the prospect of further anti-Semitism. These newcomers were mainly rural workers, in contrast to the urban Jewish community of the East End. A triple-pronged plan was launched, to dissuade more refugees from entering Britain, remove those who had already entered the overcrowded East End and integrate them into English Judaism and society.

**Chronic overcrowding** The East End by the late 1880s was chronically overcrowded. Families of three generations would cram into two rooms and often take in a lodger. Conditions were often unsanitary, and the sudden influx following the Russian pogroms exacerbated the situation.

The one person who had the biggest effect on highlighting the desperate state of living conditions in the East End was Jack the Ripper. Having murdered at least five women in 1888, and never been caught, his crime spree shone a light on the conditions of slum housing in the East End. The impetus to clear slum dwellings accelerated. The Ripper, it was thought by some, may have been Jewish. Several police suspects lived in the area, but were never charged.

**The Aliens Act** The 'foreign' population in what became the Borough of Stepney (which included Spitalfields and Whitechapel) numbered about 16,000 in 1881. By 1899, there were around 125,000 Jewish people living in the borough.

Housing, health and social issues became a serious matter. There were calls for immigration to be halted, including by the MP for Stepney, Major William Gordon Evans. Warnings were issued that such levels of immigration were changing the ways of life in these areas and, consequently, forcing English-born dwellers out.

A Royal Commission was created in 1902 and included on the panel was Lord Rothschild. To establish the facts, many Jewish people were called to give evidence. The resulting 1905 Aliens Act prohibited the movement of known criminals and paupers into Britain, though it did preserve the right to political asylum.

In 1911, following a botched jewellery robbery *(page 47)* in Houndsditch, two men were cornered in a house on Sidney Street. This triggered certain sections of the press to demand further amendments to the Aliens Act, as they claimed this event showed that foreign anarchists and criminals were running wild in London, killing policeman. With the outbreak of the First World War, however, immigration was reduced almost to zero.

**The East End Exodus** Around the beginning of the nineteenth century most Jewish people, regardless of wealth, were living in the East End, with the poorest living in the areas around Brick Lane and Middlesex Street. By the 1840s, the wealthier middle classes began to move out to the north and west of London: Finsbury Square, Islington and Bayswater. After the Second World War, many who had been evacuated never returned and the Jewish population halved to 30,000. Some began new lives in the suburbs of Golders Green, St Johns Wood, East Ham and Walthamstow. Today the Jewish population in the East End is less than 3,000.

Members of the Jewish community that grew up in the East End and elsewhere, have gone on to contribute hugely to life in Britain. Jewish philanthropists including the Rothschild and Montefiore families have made huge contributions to social care and housing projects, not only in the East End but all over Britain. Despite the deprivation of East End life, numerous Jewish artists, musicians, doctors and lawyers flourished. These included the poets Isaac Rosenberg and Siegfried Sassoon, the artist Mark Gertler, the playwright Israel Zangwill and the media impresario Lew Grade. Of the Jewish-owned factories that have provided affordable attire and food for the working and middle classes, some, such as Moss Bros, Tesco and Marks & Spencer, have gone on to become high street household names.

*Far left: a child refugee of the Russian pogroms arrives at Tilbury Dock. Above: Tesco and Marks & Spencer shopping bags.*

# THE CITY

*Total walking distance 1.5km*

This walk, through the very heart of the City of London, takes you where the first community of Jewish people settled in the eleventh century. Life was far from comfortable for the new arrivals as they faced hostility. Centuries later it would be the accomplishments of several prominent Jewish bankers that really put the City on the global financial map.

***1* The Mikveh** At the beginning of the twenty-first century an archaeological dig unearthed a 700-year-old mikveh at 1-6 Milk Street. These streets were the location of the first Jewish community in London. A mikveh is a Jewish ritual bath, used to achieve spiritual purity by immersion, often before religious events such as Yom Kippur or Shabbat. Orthodox Jewish women are required to bathe in the mikveh after their period or childbirth.

The house containing the mikveh was owned by Moses Crespin, a Jewish financier. In 1290, all Jewish people living in England were banished from the country.

The Christian family who took over the house on Milk Street probably had the bath filled in and buried. Following the unearthing of the mikveh, it was dismantled, removed from the site and is now on display at the Jewish Museum in north London.

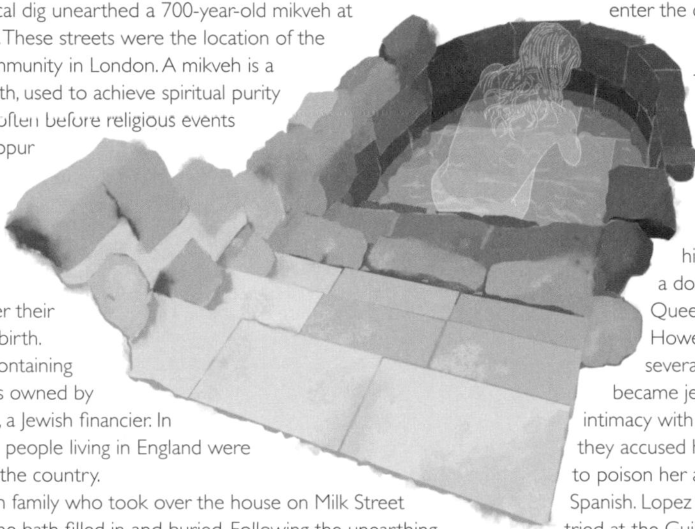

*Left to right: a mikveh, unearthed in the City and now on display in the Jewish Museum; a 1930s poster for Moss Bros; a ceramic sign marking the site of the Great Synagogue in Old Jewry.*

**2 Rodrigo Lopez** The site of the current Guildhall was once a Roman amphitheatre. The Guildhall was established in 1440, as the administrative centre for the City of London. Following the Great Fire of 1666 and German bombings raids in 1940, the building has undergone many repairs. The medieval building also served as the Courts of Justice and it was here, in 1593, that Rodrigo Lopez was tried for treason.

At the time of the coronation of Elizabeth I in 1558, many Sephardic Jews of the Iberian Peninsula were fleeing to avoid the Inquisitions, a small number of them illegally entering England (it would be another hundred years before Jewish people could legally enter the country).

Rodrigo Lopez was a Portuguese-born, Jewish physician who, because of his skills and conversion to Catholicism, was allowed to enter England legally in 1559. He was successful in treating several noblemen of the time, including Sir Francis Walsingham and the Earl of Essex. As a result of his fame and work as a doctor, Lopez became Queen Elizabeth's physician. However, there were several courtiers who became jealous of Lopez's intimacy with the Queen, and they accused him of attempting to poison her and of spying for the Spanish. Lopez was arrested and tried at the Guildhall on the grounds of treason. In early 1594, he was found guilty and was hung, drawn and quartered at Tyburn.

It is believed that Shakespeare used Lopez as inspiration for the character of Shylock in his play *The Merchant of Venice.*

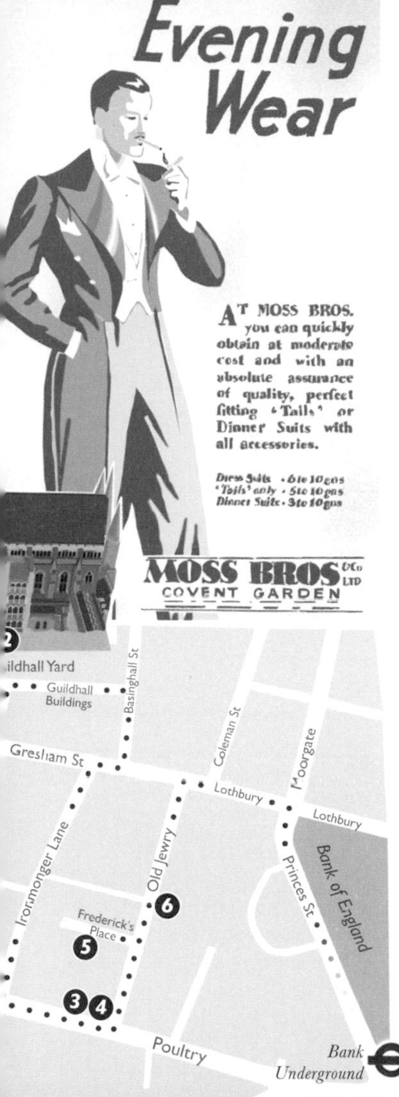


**3 Moss Bros.** At 83 Cheapside is a branch of Moss Bros.; one of 100 such stores in the UK. This clothing company was founded by Moses Moss who, in 1851, opened two shops in Covent Garden that sold second-hand clothing. Moss had begun his working life as a rag and bone man. The company expanded and later moved into producing formal menswear and hiring suits. In 1898, the shops, now managed by two sons of Moses, was rebranded as Moss Bros.

**4 1262 Massacre** On the corner of Old Jewry and Cheapside once stood St Mary Colechurch and it was here, in 1262, that an argument between a Christian and a Jewish money lender over rates of interest occurred. Matters quickly escalated into a riot in which Jewish houses and a synagogue were destroyed. It is claimed that over 500 Jewish people were killed in the attack.

Hostility towards the Jewish community had increased towards the end of the twelfth century, as they were the only people allowed to lend money and control the rate of interest. Medieval Christians were unable to lend money with interest. In the riots, numerous accounting ledgers were destroyed and with that, the money owed to the Jewish people was negated. Within 30 years they would be, by royal decree, banished from England for nearly 350 years.

**5 Disraeli the solicitor** From 1821, for three years, Benjamin Disraeli *(page 51)* worked at 6 Frederick's Place while articled to a City law firm.

**6 The Great Synagogue** Not long after William I arrived in London, he encouraged a group of Jewish financiers and their families from Rouen, France, to

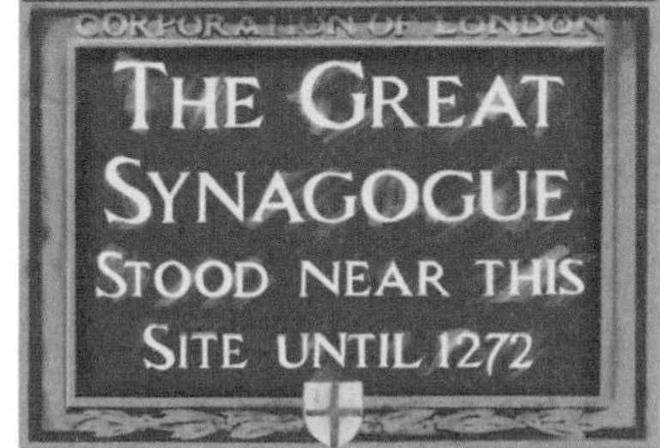


come to England and assist the Crown with its fiscal acumen, in order to finance the army and defences such as the Tower of London. Soon a small Jewish community developed in this area of the City with a school, shops and a kosher butcher. In 1230, the first 'great' synagogue was created for their spiritual needs and a plaque marks the location of the building. Prior to this date, Jewish people would have celebrated the Sabbath in the privacy of their own homes. In 1272, Henry III instigated charges against the them and seized one-third of their moveable assets. The Great Synagogue was closed and handed over to the brothers of St Anthony of Vienna.

Walking these pages 0.9km

**1 The Mansion House** The monarch was (and still is) the head of the Church of England and even by the start of the nineteenth century its members alone (i.e. only those baptised) could hold senior positions with the state. So consequently, Jews, Roman Catholics and non-conformists in Britain were barred from high office. Jewish people could not be barristers, MPs or study at Oxford or Cambridge. By 1829, the Catholic Emancipation Act was introduced, which then gave Catholics greater access to employment within state-run bodies.

Many Jewish people at the time preferred not to agitate for further reforms, fearing a rise in anti-Semitism. In 1830, it was decreed that anyone could become a freeman of the City of London, after taking an oath in their preferred religion. In 1835, David Salomons, founder of Westminster Bank, became the first Jewish Sheriff of London and 20 years later he became the first Jewish Lord Mayor of London.

When Marcus Samuel, a founder of Shell Transport (later Royal Dutch Shell), became mayor in 1902, the ceremonial Lord Mayor's Show paraded through the streets of Whitechapel to show the many Jewish refugees that they could make it to the top.

*Clockwise from left: Nathan Mayer Rothschild; the Mansion House; pugilist Daniel Mendoza; the five arrows that form the Rothschild's banking symbol: the arrows represent the five sons of Mayer Amschel Rothschild.*

**2 N M Rothschild & Sons** In New Court, just off St Swithin's Lane, Nathan Mayer Rothschild established his family home and bank. His father, Mayer Amschel Rothschild of Frankfurt, Germany, despatched four of his five sons to different European cities to establish businesses.

In 1798, at the age of 21, Nathan moved to Manchester and founded a textile company. Within six years he had moved to London and commenced trading on the London Stock Exchange. Then, in 1809 he founded the investment bank, N M Rothschild & Sons.

The family's connections across Europe were hugely influential and in a time of pigeon post, Nathan was able to give Prime Minister Lord Liverpool news of the British victory at Waterloo 30 hours before Wellington's official despatch from the front, and the government was able to use this knowledge to its financial advantage.

Following the death of Nathan in 1836, his son Lionel de Rothschild *(page 51)* took over as head of the bank.

N M Rothschild & Sons invested heavily in British government bonds, and assisted with the British acquisition of the Suez Canal *(page 51)* and numerous other business ventures. The extended Rothschild family also became hugely influential in many philanthropic schemes *(page 37)*.

The independent investment bank is still at the same address today, though the building has recently been reconstructed.

Princes St

Poultry

Walbrook

St Stephen's Row

St Stephen Walbrook

Mansion House Place

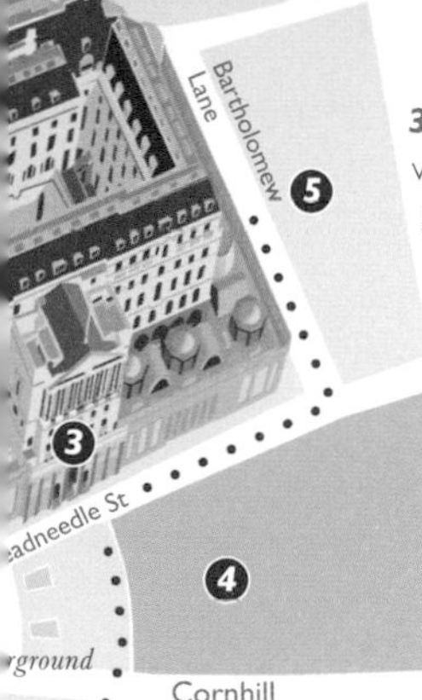


**3 The Bank of England** The Bank of England was founded in 1694 to enable the English government to raise cheap loans and rebuild the navy, following defeat by the French in 1690. It was also empowered to issue bank notes and coins. The Bank of England was privately owned until after the Second World War when it was nationalised, though since 1998, it has become an independent public administration. In 1868, Alfred de Rothschild became the first Jewish director of the Bank of England *(page 17)*.

**4 The Royal Exchange** The Royal Exchange was founded by Sir Thomas Gresham as a much-needed centre of commerce and trade within the City of London. The building was opened by Elizabeth I in 1571. Initially, brokers dealt in physical goods and stocks, but later insurance deals were traded here. It also became an early covered shopping centre when shops were introduced to the Exchange (a forerunner of the upmarket retail and restaurant hub that is present today).

A hundred years later, of the 124 licensed brokers in the Royal Exchange, only 12 could be Jewish. Samson Gideon became one of the 'twelve' in 1729. Gideon was a shrewd businessman and helped navigate the English government out of the South Sea Bubble fiasco with what would be today a £630 million loan. In 1745, during the Jacobite rebellion, Gideon again came to the rescue with further loans as government stock collapsed.

The brothers-in-law Nathan Mayer Rothschild and Moses Montefiore both traded here and established the Alliance Assurance company, which would later become Sun Alliance Insurance.

The Royal Exchange played an instrumental part in enhancing the City of London as an international trading centre.

**5 Daniel Mendoza's boxing academy** In Capel Court (the street no longer exists) once stood Daniel Mendoza's boxing academy. The school was established in 1787, after the Prince of Wales (the future King George IV) witnessed Mendoza beat an opponent in just ten rounds and awarded him £500. Mendoza once went 118 rounds to beat Harry the Coalheaver. Bare-knuckled bouts ended when one of the boxers was either knocked out or conceded.

Mendoza was born in 1764 to a Sephardic family living in Whitechapel. He fought under the title of 'Mendoza the Jew'. With his slight frame and height, he adopted a more scientific approach, employing skilful footwork and a defensive stance. In 1792, Mendoza became the British boxing champion. His contribution to raising the profile of British Jewry was immense.

# SPITALFIELDS

*Total walking distance 3.5km*

This small area, east of the City, was once home to a hospital, St Mary Spital, and from this it became Spital Fields. Following the development of the district after the Great Fire of 1666, many waves of immigrants chose to live in the area, including Jewish people fleeing the persecution and pogroms in Eastern Europe. Though this group have now largely departed, there remains many signs of their former presence in Spitalfields.

**1 Kindertransport Memorial** In 1938, Nicholas Winton, the son of Jewish parents, having witnessed the horrendous conditions endured by Jewish people in Prague, campaigned to evacuate Jewish children from Czechoslovakia to Britain. Following the night of 9–10 November 1938 (later known as Kristallnacht), when Jewish property all over Germany was attacked and 30,000 Jewish people arrested, Winton's campaign intensified. Starting a month later a group of Jewish children were despatched from Berlin by train towards the Belgian ports and ultimately Liverpool Street station. More evacuations followed from other parts of Germany and its occupied states. Of the 10,000 children evacuated to the UK, 80 per cent would never see their parents again, as they perished in the Nazi death camps. One fortunate escapee was the sculptor and architect Frank Meisler. Later in life, he was commissioned to create a memorial to the Kindertransport.

In 2006, a cast bronze sculpture of five children with luggage, entitled *The Arrival,* was unveiled. It stands in Hope Square at Liverpool Street station. A smaller, second sculpture, created by Flor Kent, is also dedicated to the Kindertransport and can be seen at the same station.

**2 The Jewish Board of Guardians** The Jewish Board of Guardians (JBG) was established in 1859, to amalgamate several Ashkenazi charities into one collective and more effective group. Its offices were eventually established on Middlesex Street in what is now The Astronomer pub (a plaque marks the location). Led by the banker Lionel Louis Cohen, the process of relief was moved away from individual synagogues and towards a unified organisation, with paid employees to assist the JBG assessment volunteers. The Board loaned money to enable Jewish tradespeople to rent equipment such as sewing machines and woodworking tools to generate a means of income. The JBG would also challenge landlords who were not looking after their tenants correctly, ensuring broken windows were repaired and damp problems fixed. Newly arrived Jewish migrants had to wait six months before they could apply for assistance, as the JBG did not want to appear to be encouraging immigration, especially following the 1881 assassination of the Russian Tsar Alexander II, when a trickle of Jewish immigrants became a deluge.

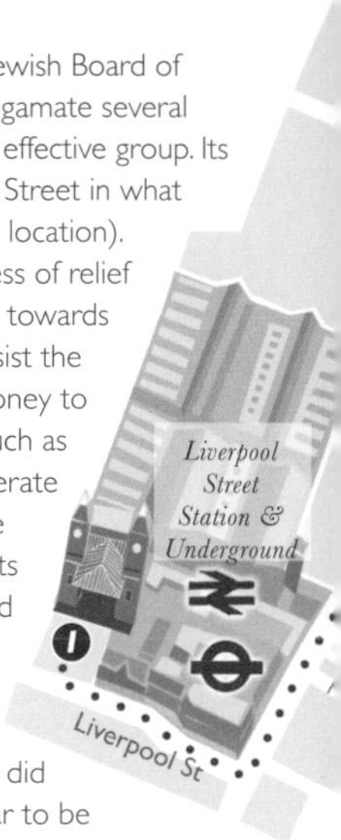

**3 Sandy's Row Synagogue** This modest structure in a quiet, narrow street in Spitalfields has been a place of worship for over 250 years. The Huguenots created the building, L'Église de L'Artillerie, in 1766 *(page 14)*; later it became home to several groups of Baptists, and in 1867, it became a synagogue. It is the oldest, functioning Ashkenazi temple in London.

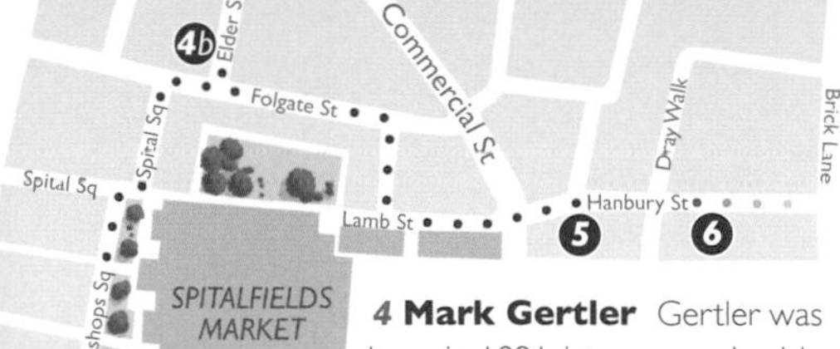


**4 Mark Gertler** Gertler was born in 1891, into a poor Jewish family living at 16 Gun Street (**4a**, *now under Spitalfields Market*). After winning several art prizes in his late teens and with sponsorship, Gertler spent four years at the Slade School of Fine Art, where he met fellow Jewish artist Isaac Rosenberg *(page 39)* plus up-and-coming painters; Paul Nash and Stanley Spencer. By 1912, he was living on the top floor at 32 Elder Street (**4b**, a plaque marks the house) While visiting the Easter Fair on Hampstead Heath three years later, he became fascinated with the attractions and began to make sketches of them. In 1916, he had completed the *Merry-Go-Round* painting. It featured uniformed military figures on leave, accompanied by women, with storm clouds looming above. It became known as Gertler's most famous anti-war painting. In the same year he was obliged to attend an army recruitment office, but Gertler, a pacifist, was rejected because of his mother's Austrian birth. After the war, he continued to paint despite bouts of tuberculosis. He found many personal relationships difficult to maintain and, following a failed marriage, the death of his mother and a disastrous exhibition, he died by gassing himself in 1939.

**5 Bud Flanagan** Bud was born Chaim Reuben Weintrop at 12 Hanbury Street in 1896. His parents had earlier fled Poland to avoid a pogrom. In 1915, Weintrop signed up to fight with the British army in France and it was here that he encountered the anti-Semitic Sergeant-Major Flanagan from whom he took his stage name. 'Flanagan' is probably best known for his music hall double act with Chesney Allen, leader of the Crazy Gang and for their song 'Underneath the Arches'.

**6 Eleanor Marx** Eleanor, the youngest daughter of Karl Marx, was born in 1855. Although of Jewish ancestry, she, like her father, was not brought up as a Jew. However, she did learn Yiddish to enable her to reach out and organise Jewish workers' groups of the East End and, unlike her father, she did mix with the proletariat. In 1885, Marx helped found the Socialist League, along with Edward Aveling (her common-law husband), William Morris and Annie Beasant. Beasant was assisted by Marx three years later when organising the Bryant & May matchgirls strike. Marx was also involved in the London Dock strike of 1889. She spoke many times at Hanbury Hall on the subject of workers' rights. In 1895, Marx addressed a conference at the Great Assembly Hall *(page 44)* against the racist resolution of the TUC that had called for the exclusion of 'aliens', including eastern European Jewish migrants. Sadly, Eleanor Marx died by suicide at the age of 43 following the discovery that Aveling had taken another lover.

*Clockwise from far left: the Kindertransport Memorial created by Frank Meisler at Liverpool Street station; Merry-Go-Round (1916) by Mark Gertler; a Delph mezuzah at Sandy Row Synagogue; Eleanor Marx, socialist and feminist activist.*

***1*** **19 Princelet Street** Samuel Worrall, master carpenter to the architect Nicholas Hawksmoor, built this early Georgian house in 1718. By the 1740s, it was occupied by a wealthy Protestant Huguenot family, the Ogiers. The Ogier family had fled France following persecution by the Catholics *(page 14)*. In 1870, long after many Huguenots had moved away, the building was converted into an Ashkenazi synagogue. The back of the house was extended out to form a two-level temple and it became a very popular shul for many Jewish people in the area. By the 1950s, the synagogue was in a poor state of repair, the local Jewish population had begun to move away, and by 1963, it had officially closed. 19 Princelet Street regained attention in 1980, when a sealed-up room above the synagogue was broken into, revealing the papers, writings and books of its former caretaker and scholar, David Rodinsky. Rodinsky had disappeared 11 years earlier. Now under the ownership of The Spitalfields Centre, the house is slowly being repaired and restored and will become a museum of immigration and diversity; a fine tribute to the waves of immigrants who settled in Spitalfields.

**2 Hebrew Dramatic Club** In 1883, the actor Jacob Adler fled the Russian pogroms. Within three years he had converted the house at 6 Princelet Street (now marked number 8) into a Yiddish theatre with an audience capacity of 500. The following year, 17 people died in a stampede at the theatre when a false fire alarm was raised. There is a pavement plaque outside what was the theatre, though this is a tribute to the viola player Lionel Tertis, who lived at 8 Princelet Street. His father was a reader at the synagogue at number 19.

***3*** **Ghost signs** Although there are no longer large numbers of Jewish people living in Spitalfields, there are still numerous reminders of its past occupants. At 4 Wilkes Street (**3a**) is the hand-painted sign for H. Suskin (Textile) Ltd, even though it ceased trading years ago. 92 Brick Lane (**3b**) was a shop owned by Ch N. Katz until the1990s. It sold mainly paper bags and twine. It is now an art gallery, however the painted sign above the window still remains. At Christ Church School at 47 Brick Lane (**3c**), a small Star of David can be seen on a black rainwater pipe.

**4 Fournier Street** During the eighteenth century, wealthy Huguenot weavers and their families occupied most of the housing shown on these pages. Occupancy per three- or four-storey house was often as low as three people. By 1851, things had changed dramatically. The Census Report of that year revealed that at 23 Fournier Street 18 people or three families including, in some instances, a servant or two, occupied the house. Eighteen years after the Russian pogroms and the subsequent flow of immigrants to the capital, a map of Jewish East London revealed that Fournier Street was 95 to 100 per cent Jewish-occupied.

However, the house in Fournier Street later shifted away from multiple occupancy towards single, large family occupancy. The Booth Poverty map (1889) showed the street to be 'Fairly comfortable. Good ordinary earnings/Middle class. Well-to-do'. However, Fournier Street was not typical of the area; poverty and destitution were still rife in Spitalfields.

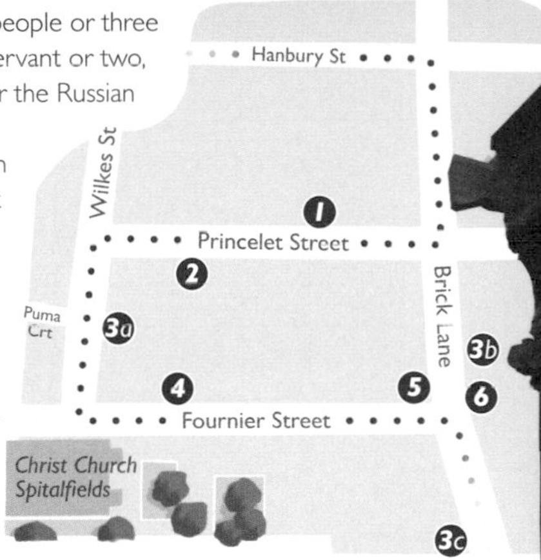

**5 Machzike Hadath Synagogue** The mid-eighteenth century building on the corner of Fournier Street and Brick Lane neatly encapsulates the flow of immigrants through Spitalfields. It was built as a French Protestant chapel in 1743 to serve the spiritual needs of the Huguenot immigrants *(page 14)*. In 1809, it was briefly a centre for converting Jewish people to Christianity, before becoming a Methodist chapel in 1819. The Machzike Hadath community bought the building in 1898 to convert it into a synagogue. This ultra-orthodox group of Jews from Lithuania were unhappy with the relaxed approach to worship taken by the Anglo-Jews. Relations came to a head on Yom Kippur 1904, when secular Jewish anarchists pelted the fasting congregation with bacon sandwiches as they left the synagogue, and a riot ensued. By the 1960s, the Jewish population of the East End had declined so far that the building was sold in 1975, and was reopened as the Brick Lane Jamme Masjid Mosque the following year.

**6 Russian Vapour Baths** At 86 Brick Lane there once existed a vapour (or steam) baths. Jewish men, usually immigrants from Eastern Europe, would attend the baths, especially before Friday prayers. On Wednesdays, women were allowed to use the facilities. The baths were better known locally as 'Schewzik's' after the Russian owner, Rabbi Benjamin Schewzik. In the late nineteenth century there were at least four more vapour baths operating in the East End. Schewzik's was destroyed by fire in 1940, though not as a result of bombing.

*Clockwise from far left: the hand-painted hanging sign of Suskin Ltd; the exterior of 19 Princelet Street; the pavement plaque commemorating the international viola player Lionel Tertis, located outside 8 Princelet Street; an enamel sign advertising the Russian Vapour Baths in Brick Lane; the Star of David on a rainwater pipe at Christ Church School in Brick Lane; the 'ghost-sign' for the former shop of Ch N. Katz.*

Walking these pages 0.5km

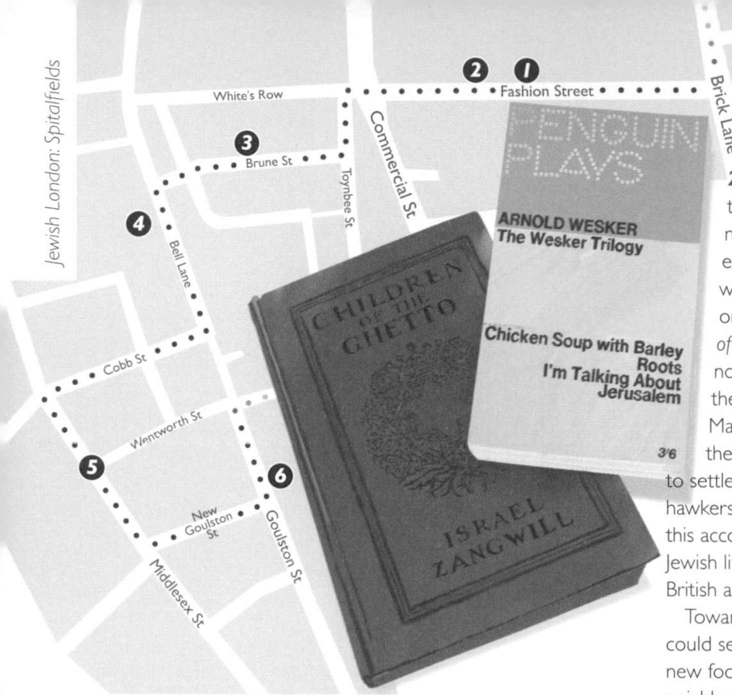

*Clockwise from left: Book covers of Arnold Wesker and Israel Zangwill's bestsellers; the Petticoat Lane Sunday market circa 1910; the facia of the soup kitchen. The year the building opened is displayed above the portal in both the Hebrew and Gregorian calendars.*

**1 Arnold Wesker** The author and playwright Arnold Wesker was born in 1932, to socialist Jewish parents and lived as a child at 43 Fashion Street. After leaving school he worked as a kitchen porter, pastry chef and a furniture maker before embarking on a career as a writer. In his second play, *Chicken Soup with Barley*, written in 1958, Wesker told the story of the disintegration of a political ideology and an East End Jewish family, the Kahn's, over a 20-year period. The play, the first part of the very successful Wesker trilogy, opens in 1936 with the Cable Street Riots *(page 49)* and ends in 1956 with the Soviet invasion of Hungary. Wesker went on to write 50 plays in his lifetime and was knighted in 2008 for 'services to drama'. He died in 2016, aged 83.

**2 Israel Zangwill** Wesker was not the only author to have lived on Fashion Street. Israel Zangwill was born nearby in 1864 and lived here for a while as a child. He was educated at the nearby Jews' Free School (**4**), where he would later teach. Zangwill became a great observer of life on the streets of the Jewish East End. His book *The Children of the Ghetto: A Study of a Peculiar People*, published in 1892, notes the struggles (and cheerfulness) of the workers and their families crammed into squalid tenements and houses. Many were largely impoverished Jewish people who had fled the pogroms of Eastern Europe in the early 1880s and began to settle as best they could in the East End of London, working as hawkers, craftsmen and small-scale manufacturers. Zangwill wrote this account as an insider, presenting a more rounded account of Jewish life in the area, unlike so many other reports written by British authors and journalists.

Towards the end of the nineteenth century, the East End could seem like another world to the other local Londoners: new foods and the use of Yiddish dominated these streets. The neighbourhood included the rookeries of Flower and Dean Street, where several of Jack the Ripper's victims had resided. Yet despite this connection to one of the most notorious murderers in London, there was very little violence or drunkenness. Zangwill, once nicknamed 'the Dickens of the Ghetto', would become a supporter of women's rights and a campaigner for a homeland for Jewish people.

**3 Jewish Soup Kitchen** A Jewish soup kitchen was first established in 1854 in Leman Street as a way to assist hungry and needy Jewish people, especially during cold periods and times of economic hardship. Such philanthropic institutions were nothing new in this area of London. In 1797, the Spitalfields Soup Society had been established to feed the families of unemployed weavers. With the influx of impoverished Jewish people from Eastern Europe in the 1880s, the need for kosher facilities grew. The Soup Kitchen relocated to Brune Street in 1903. But to earn a meal of meat soup and bread, a chit had to be obtained from the Board of Guardians *(page 30)*. Following the decline of the Jewish population in the area the establishment closed in 1992. The building and its facia still survive.

**4 Jews' Free School** In 1732, a Talmud Torah (Hebrew school) was established within the Great Synagogue, Dukes Place. It would later become the Jews' Free School (JFS). In 1800, there were no free Jewish schools in the East End, so many poor Jewish children would attend the local Christian schools at the risk of conversion to Christianity. The JFS was established in 1817 with donations from wealthy Jewish families, including the Rothschilds and Mayers. It quickly became successful, resulting in a move to larger premises on Bell Lane in 1822. By 1900, with over 4,000 pupils, it was the largest school in Europe. It was able to take hundreds of young children from Eastern Europe and turn them into English speaking young men and women who would be welcome in 'respectable' society. Among those who attended the school were Bud Flanagan *(page 31)* and Israel Zangwill. Following the Second World War the JFS relocated and is now situated in Kenton, north-west London.

**5 Petticoat Lane Market** By the late nineteenth century Petticoat Lane Market was largely a Jewish market held on a Sunday, and a place to buy and sell old clothing and second-hand goods. In 1830, the street's name was changed to Middlesex Street, although it is still known as the 'Petticoat Lane' market today, although most of the Jewish traders have long departed. The travel writer Henry Morton patronisingly described the market in 1925 as '*a Cairo, Baghdad, Jeruselem, Aleppo, Tunis or Tangier… only a penny ride from Ludgate Hill*'.

**6 Ripper Graffiti** Following the murder of Catherine Eddowes by Jack the Ripper in September 1888, a chalked message was found in Goulston Street. It read: '*The Juwes are the men that will not be blamed for nothing*'. The graffiti may have been written by a Jew annoyed that they, as a race, were being accused of the murders, or by the Ripper himself, who left Eddowes' bloodied apron at the site to confuse the investigations. The murders were so horrific that many found it hard to believe they could be the work of an Englishman. Anti-Semitism was running high and several local Jewish men were accused of the murders, although they were never charged.

*Walking these pages 0.9km*

**1 The First Board School 1871** In 1870, the Education Act was successfully passed through Parliament. This required every child from the ages of 5 to 13 in England and Wales to receive a free education. Prior to this, education was haphazard with some being provided by the church, and even then attendance was voluntary.

A new Board School was created on Old Castle Street for children of all faiths and it was expected that Jewish children would flock to it. However, many Jewish parents believed that the new school would be missionary in nature and so avoided sending their children there, preferring instead to send their offspring to Jewish schools or keep them at home to work in the family business. This issue of resistance was overcome when the Board School appointed the headmaster of a nearby Jewish school, Abraham Levy, as headmaster. Within a short space of time 95 per cent of the Board Schools' intake was Jewish. Although Old Castle Street was a state school, it still recognised Jewish holidays, and in winter, children were dismissed early on Fridays to prepare for the Sabbath.

**2 Toynbee Hall** Canon Samuel Barnett, vicar of St Jude's parish, Whitechapel, believed that indiscriminate charity was a curse, as the recipients would never learn to work or save for themselves. So it was no surprise that many of the East End poor turned to the Salvation Army or other charitable groups for handouts. Barnett believed in moral improvement through education, not food parcels, so he and his wife, Henrietta, established a small school for both children and adults. Lessons included vocational skills that could be useful in gaining employment. Trips were arranged for children who had never ventured beyond the East End to visit the country and seaside. In 1884, the Barnetts established Toynbee Hall on Commercial Street as a permanent education centre for the poor of the East End. Young, middle-class Oxbridge graduates assisted with the programmes of education, culture and art. Unlike many charities operating in the area, Toynbee Hall was strictly non-sectarian, despite being established by a Christian priest, and was regarded as a settlement.

The building, which still stands, was designed to appear like a red-brick university building of its day, with an entrance through a quadrangle. Included among the many volunteers were William Beveridge and Clement Attlee. Both were influenced by their time at Toynbee Hall and would later go on to transform the social and welfare system of the country. Toynbee Hall is still a centre for the campaign against injustice and poverty.

*Sites of the former Nathaniel (4) and Charlotte de Rothschild Dwellings (3)*

FP

Flower and Dean Wk

Thrawl St

Wentworth St

Old Castle St

Commercial St

Pomell Way

*Aldgate Undergr*

Whitechapel

*From left to right: Toynbee Hall; the Charlotte de Rothschild Dwelling Arch that was removed from the building during demolition in the 1970s and rebuilt on Wentworth Street; Abe Saperstein, founder of the Harlem Globetrotters.*

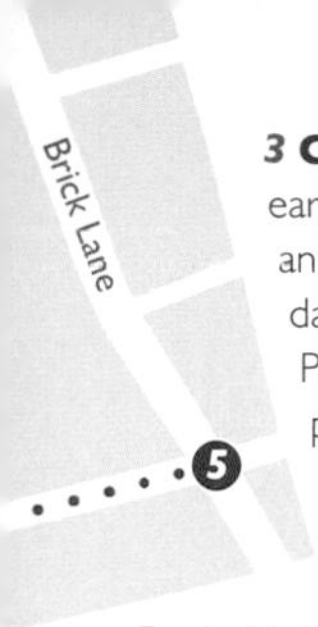

Brick Lane

**3 Charlotte de Rothschild Dwellings** Since the early eighteenth century, housing in the East End had been an issue. Many tenements and houses were overcrowded, damp and infested. Following the pogroms in Russia and Poland in the 1880s, many thousands of displaced Jewish people from eastern Europe arrived in East London. In 1884, a report by the Jewish Board of Guardians into the state of housing inspired a group of philanthropic Jewish people including Frederick Mocatta, Claude Montefiore, Samuel Montague, with Lord Nathan Mayer de Rothschild as chairman, to establish the Four Per Cent Industrial Dwellings Company (IDC) to build safe and decent housing for the working classes with low rents and a 4 per cent return per annum for investors. There was concern among the Anglo-Jewry that this sudden influx of immigrants could result in a serious backlash if nothing was done to assist them. The first dwelling, a six-storey structure, was built on part of the Flower and Dean rookery, north of Wentworth Street and named after Lord Rothschild's mother, Charlotte. It was a safe and habitable construction with running water, and contained nearly 200 flats. The average rent charged was about 5 shillings, which was much lower than that charged by the nearby Peabody Estates. The new tenants were mainly Jewish immigrants.

By 1901, the IDC, with further development, had housed over 4,500 people in the East End. The Charlotte de Rothschild Dwellings were demolished in the 1970s, though one of the portals was rebuilt as a memorial on Wentworth Street (**3a**) *(Four of Jack the Ripper's victims had lived, at some point, in Flower & Dean Street rookery (the street no longer exists). The horrific murders would shine a light on the deplorable conditions to be found in the East End.)*

**4 Abe Saperstein and the Harlem Globetrotters** 
Abe Saperstein was born in the Nathaniel Dwellings in 1902, to a Jewish family from Poland. At the age of five his family moved to Chicago and while at school Saperstein, despite his height (1.6m), developed a talent for playing many sports, especially basketball. He established, managed and played for the Chicago Reds and through this he went on to meet Walter Ball, a black baseball player, who recruited Saperstein as a booking agent for his team. By the late 1920s, Saperstein had built a new basketball team called the New York Harlem Globetrotters. Despite not being from Harlem, Saperstein wanted everyone to know that they were a black basketball team. The Globetrotters amalgamated basketball with showmanship and went on to become international stars, playing both competitively and purely for entertainment. Saperstein fought against racial segregation and saw the Globetrotters and other teams become accepted as black players within a once white-dominated National Basketball Association.

**5 Brick Lane** Brick Lane was from the 1880s until the 1930s the spine of a large Jewish community. Virtually every shop on the Lane catered for this group, including hairdressers, tailors, printers, cobblers, and delis such as the 24-hours Beigel Bake and the famous Bloom's Restaurant. Yiddish was predominant both in speech and signage.

*Walking these pages 0.8km*

# WHITECHAPEL

***Total walking distance 2.9km***

Whitechapel Road was the cultural and religious geographic spine of the Jewish community during the late nineteenth and early twentieth centuries.

***1* The Star of David** This ornate Star of David insignia *(above)* is located above Alberts Menswear shop door and is just to the right of the archway leading to Gunthorpe Street. It marks the site of the former offices and printing presses of the *Jewish Daily Post*, which had a short-lived reign here from 1934 to 1935. The paper struggled to complete with *The Jewish Times* and was sued by a rabbi following the publication of a misleading article about him. The metal sign, once painted gold, was created by one of the paper's cartoonists, Arthur Szyk. It features two sword-wielding rampant lions supporting the Star of David.

***2* The anarchists of Angel Alley** Less than 20m away from the Star of David is a narrow passage way, Angel Alley. It is here that the Freedom Bookshop is located and just to the left of the shop entrance is a commissioned artwork, created by Anya Patel, that depicts 36 anarchists – painters, musicians, writers and politicians, including well-known Jewish anarchists: Noam Chomsky, Alexander Berkman and Emma Goldman.

***3* Whitechapel Art Gallery** During the 1880s, the philanthropists Samuel and Henrietta Barnett frequently held art exhibitions in St Jude's Church next to Toynbee Hall *(page 36)*. The Barnetts founded this art gallery on Whitechapel Road in 1901, with the aim of bringing art to the people of the East End and an escape for many from the dark and dirty streets of the East End. The gallery would open its doors on Sunday afternoons, the day after the Sabbath (or Shabbat), especially to enable local Jewish people to visit. Charles Harrison Townsend designed the Art Nouveau gallery with its dominant sandstone façade and arch. It was, and still is, a dominant feature of Whitechapel Road and an alternative art gallery to those located in west and central London.

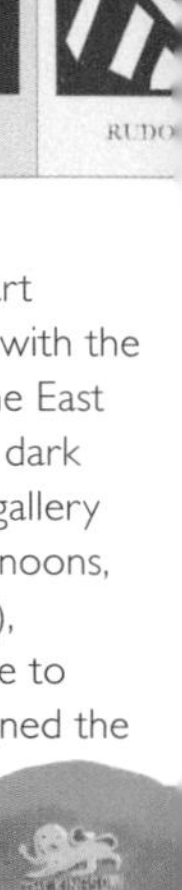

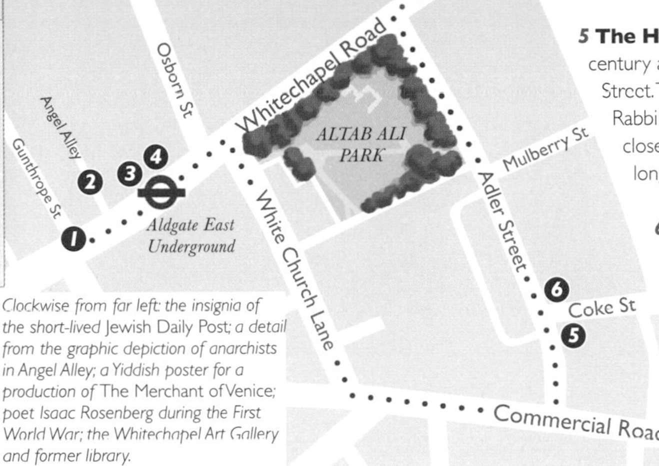


*Clockwise from far left: the insignia of the short-lived Jewish Daily Post; a detail from the graphic depiction of anarchists in Angel Alley; a Yiddish poster for a production of* The Merchant of Venice*; poet Isaac Rosenberg during the First World War; the Whitechapel Art Gallery and former library.*

**5 The Hambro Synagogue** At the end of the nineteenth century a new Hambro synagogue was consecrated on Adler Street. The street (formerly Union Street) was named after Chief Rabbi Hermann Adler (1839–1911). In 1936, the synagogue closed and merged with the Great Synagogue. The structure no longer exists and a new development sits on the site.

**6 New Yiddish Theatre** This theatre opened in 1936 within the Adler Hall as the New Jewish Theatre. The building had previously housed the Israel Friendly Society, a boxing ring and a ballroom. In 1943, it was rebranded as the New Yiddish Theatre but was forced to move to Stoke Newington due to an unsafe roof. It was a relative latecomer to the world of Yiddish East End theatre. One of its better known productions was a Yiddish version of Shakespeare's *The Merchant of Venice* starring Meier Tzelniker as Shylock and his daughter, Anna, as Portia. She stated '*Jewish immigrants needed the Yiddish theatre for their souls, just as they needed bread to eat*'. The use of Yiddish, often the only language spoken by Jewish immigrants during the late nineteenth century, was in decline, as their children were encouraged to learn English.

Anna Tzelniker, who later appeared in the 1983 film *Yentl* with Barbra Streisand, was probably the last Yiddish-speaking actor in the UK. She died in 2012. After the Second World War, for a brief time, the building was temporary home to the Great Synagogue of Dukes Place, which had been heavily bombed. Adler Hall was eventually demolished in 1990.

**4 Whitechapel Library** In 1892, the Barnetts, with major financial contributions from the philanthropist John Passmore Edwards MP, devised and built the Whitechapel Library (Passmore Edwards would sponsor several more free libraries across London). It provided the poor of the East End with free access to books, learning and meeting rooms. The library was initially illuminated with electric lights powered by it own generator. With its large collection of Yiddish and Hebrew books, it became known to Jewish East Enders as the 'University of the Ghetto'. The library was frequented by numerous artists and writers of the area, including David Bomberg, Mark Gertler *(page 31)*, Arnold Wesker, Bernard Kops and Isaac Rosenberg. A plaque to Rosenberg, a First World War poet, is visible outside the now former library. As the demographic of the area changed in the twentieth century, so too did the range of books on offer adjust to reflect the requirements of the new arrivals. In 2005, the library merged with the Whitechapel Art Gallery next door to provide more exhibition space. The library books were transferred to the Ideas Store, further east along Whitechapel Road.

*Walking these pages 0.6km*

**1 The White Chapel** This area takes its name from a former church, St Mary Matfelon, which stood in what is now Altab Ali Park. The medieval incarnation was painted with whitewash and became known as the 'white chapel'. In the late nineteenth century, a third rebuild of the church, complete with tower, advertised sermons in Yiddish, in a bid to convert newly arrived Jewish people from Eastern Europe to Christianity. The church was destroyed during the Blitz and was never rebuilt.

**2 Boris Bennett Photographer** Boris Sochaczewska was born in Poland in 1900. In 1922, he arrived in London, changed his surname to Bennett and began his photographic career in the East End. His first studio was close to the Royal London Hospital and in 1933, he had moved to bigger premises at 14 Whitechapel Road. Newly married couples would arrive from the synagogue to be photographed at the studio. The wedded couple, often with a retinue of bridesmaids, were shot against stylish and glamorous Hollywoodesque backgrounds. On some Sundays up to 60 couples would arrive to be photographed and huge crowds gathered just to watch the parade. It was said that if you hadn't had your wedding photo taken by Boris Bennett then you weren't really married. The four-storey building at 14 Whitechapel Road was built in 1882, with later additions including the pastel green ceramic Art Deco detail. It is still standing although no longer a photographic studio. Bennett died in 1985.

**3 Black Lion Yard** This narrow yard (or alley) no longer exists but used to run between Whitechapel Road and Old Montague Street and took its name from the Black Lion Inn (which featured in Charles Dickens *Barnaby Rudge*). It was home to around 18 Jewish-owned jewellery shops that sold engagement and wedding rings. Bizarrely, in among the goldsmiths was a small herd of cows, which supplied fresh kosher milk. Black Lion Yard was demolished and built over in 1975.



**4 The Great Garden Street Synagogue** This street, formerly known as Great Garden Street, was, until the 1960s, a thriving Jewish hub located around the Great Garden Street Synagogue, now 7–11 Greatorex Street. The synagogue, founded in 1894, was set back from the street and was also head office for the Federation of Synagogues. The temple was rebuilt in 1972. It was a popular wedding venue in its heyday with as many as 16 marriages taking place on any one Sunday and the happy couples walking down to Boris Bennett's studio on Whitechapel Road to have their matrimonial photos taken. With a declining membership, the last service was held in 1997 and the temple closed. Several carved plaques and foundation stones from the synagogue can be seen *(right)* within the courtyard of the Business Development Centre.

**5 The Kosher Luncheon Club** This is the site of the last Kosher Luncheon Club in the East End. Many such clubs were established in the nineteenth century as soup kitchens to provide cheap, nourishing kosher food, such as barley soup, herrings and gefilte fish, to the local Jewish population. As time passed and quality of life improved for much of the community, so too did the offerings made by the clubs. This particular club was renowned for its Yiddish atmosphere and brusque service. It closed in 1994.

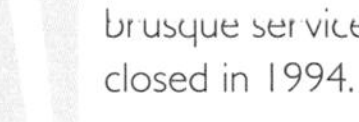


**6 Grodzinsky Bakery** In 1888, husband and wife Harris and Judith Grodzinsky left Lithuania and began selling bread from a barrow. They opened their first bakery next door to what would become the Fieldgate Street Great Synagogue. The bakery had a cellar, which ran under the temple. Following the arrival of Harris' businessman cousin Chaim Grodzinsky, the company began to expand and flourish in the 1930s. The bakery was destroyed in the Blitz.

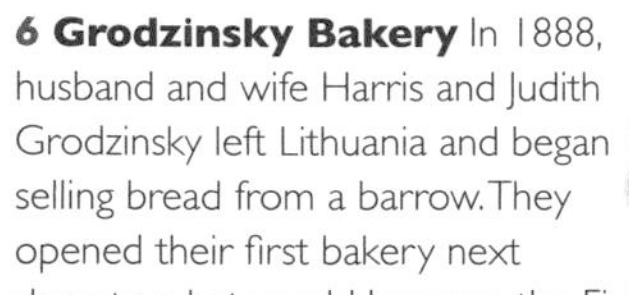

As the Jewish population of the East End began to move to the London suburbs so too did Grodzinsky bakeries. New outlets began to appear in Stamford Hill, Edgware and Golders Green. By 1965, Grodzinsky's was the largest kosher bakers in Europe and is famous for its challah (a braided bread for Jewish holidays), bagels and cakes. The Grodzinsky family are still running the company today, with additional branches in Toronto, Canada.

**7 Fieldgate Street Great Synagogue** This former synagogue on Fieldgate Street evolved out of three local, smaller Jewish temples or *shuls*. The Federation of Synagogues established this place of worship with additional funds from Nathan de Rothschild and Samuel Montagu. It opened in 1899 and was designed to accommodate 280 men on the ground floor and 240 women in the upper gallery. The building was badly damaged during the Blitz and was rebuilt after the war. Following a decline in membership from the 1980s onwards, the last service occurred in 2007 and the synagogue was sold to the East London Mosque in 2015. It is now a Zakat Centre for the processing of Muslim alms-giving. Two inscriptions, in Hebrew and English, are still in place above and to the left of the old portal.

*Clockwise from far left: an East End wedding photograph circa 1930s; the tower of St Mary's Church (once standing in Altab Ali Park) in 1900, with a banner advertising sermons in Yiddish; the inscribed lintel over the door of the former Fieldgate Street Great Synagogue; milk from the Black Lion Yard herd with a Yiddish inscription that reads* 'Fresh milk from the cows'; *a challah, a braided loaf eaten on Jewish holidays; the stone tablets from the Great Garden Street Synagogue.*

Walking these pages 0.6km

***1* Tower House** This imposing six-storey red brick structure with narrow windows was opened in 1902, to provide cheap (6d or 2.5p per night) hostel accommodation for up to 800 working men at a time. Each guest had his own room. There was also a large dining room for guests to have a meal prepared for them and the facilities to cook their own food. It was one of six such hostels devised by Montagu William Lowry-Corry, philanthropist and private secretary to Prime Minister Benjamin Disraeli *(page 51)*. Among those who stayed at this address was Joseph Stalin in 1907, while attending the 5th Congress of the Russian Social Democratic Labour Party, and in 1902, the author and journalist Jack London, who wrote *People of the Abyss* (a first-hand account of life and conditions in the East End) and who referred to Tower House as a 'monster dosshouse'.

**2 The Pavilion Theatre** Following the large influx of Jewish immigrants from Russian and Eastern Europe into the East End, after the 1881 pogroms, there was a great need to provide employment and shelter for these people. They also needed to be entertained. The Pavilion theatre was first established at 191-193 Whitechapel Road in 1828. Following a fire, several rebuilds and expansions, the seating and standing capacity rose to 3,700 by the beginning of the twentieth century and it became known as 'the Drury Lane of the East'. Though the ornate main façade was on Whitechapel Road the audience had a 50m covered walk to the auditorium.

In 1906, they began staging performances in Yiddish to cater for a new audience. Plays by Shakespeare and operas by Verdi were performed in Yiddish along with many Jewish Eastern European plays and comedies. These were often raucous events with noisy audiences shouting throughout a production. It was very successful during the 1920s. However, an attempt to convert the theatre into a cinema failed. Theatre audiences began to dwindle as the use of Yiddish diminished and many second-generation Jewish people moved away. Finally, in 1935, the theatre closed. It was damaged during the Blitz and demolished in the early 1960s. Nothing has been built on the location and it is still an empty, derelict site.

**3 Jewish Socialist Club** The Bolsheviks, having been forced out of Russia and many adjacent states by Tsar Nicholas II, assembled in London in the early twentieth century. In late April 1907, a small group including many who would later become household names – Lenin, Stalin, Gorky, Trotsky and Martov (the latter two were both Jewish) – met in secret at the Jewish Socialist Club, on the corner of Whitechapel Road and Fulbourne Street. It was here that they collected their small allowance and were informed where the Congress of the Russian Social Democratic Labour Party (RSDLP) would later meet, while being followed by Special Branch detectives and the press. The full RSDLP would meet a few days later, in a non-conformist chapel on Southgate Road, Islington, to plan the revolution in Tsarist Russia. The building on Fulbourne Street still stands.

**4 The Royal London Hospital**
The London Hospital (now the Royal London Hospital) was founded in 1740, and was originally located in Moorfields, just to the north of the City of London. In 1757, the hospital moved to a new, bigger site on Whitechapel Road and was then surrounded by fields and trees (hard to believe when standing on Whitechapel Road today). With 200 beds it was, when it opened, the largest hospital in the country, complete with rudimentary flushing toilets.

In 1783, Sir William Blizard opened a medical school within the hospital, one of the first of its kind in London. Blizard later went on to help found the Royal College of Surgeons. From its beginnings the hospital recognised the dietary needs of its Jewish patients and supplied kosher food. It also provided Jewish wards and recognised the Jewish Sabbath and festivals. The London Hospital, like many in the eighteenth and nineteenth centuries, was a voluntary hospital maintained with donations from local benefactors and the public. It received many donations from Jewish quarters. During the 1880s Lord Rothschild ensured that this tradition continued and encouraged wealthy Jewish people to make contributions. Several wards were named after Jewish benefactors: Stern, Raphael and Rothschild. These and other wards catered for the needs of Orthodox Jews. For some this was not enough, and they wanted their own Yiddish-speaking hospital *(page 46)*. Today much of the eighteenth- and nineteenth-century structure still survives, despite damage caused by a V-1 flying bomb during the Second World War.

*Clockwise from bottom left: Leon Trotsky; Tower House (as it appears today); the old Royal London Hospital with the new hospital behind; the drinking fountain donated by Jewish people of the East End in 1912; a poster for the Pavilion Theatre.*

**5 The Drinking Fountain** Loyalty to the English monarchy has always been notable among Jewish residents in Britain. In the thirteenth century they paid their taxes directly to the King in return for which they received his protection. In 1912, a drinking fountain was erected on Whitechapel Road as a memorial to Edward VII, who had died the year previously. Until the Aliens Act of 1905, many thousands of Eastern European Jewish people found refuge in the UK. The 3.5m high drinking fountain features a bas-relief image of Edward VII, complete with bronze angels and wingless cherubs (or chubby babies). Each represented an aspect of Jewish life at the time: needle and thread for the rag trade; a ship as a mode of immigration; a book representing learning and Talmudic study; and a car to represent modernity and a move away from horse-drawn wagons to motor vehicles.

The fountain also bears the inscription '*Erected from subscriptions raised by Jewish inhabitants of East London 1911*'. It was unveiled by Charles Rothschild in 1912.

N
Walking these pages 0.6km

***1* The Mile End Waste** This small strip of grass adjacent to Mile End Road, was once part of a much larger piece of land known as the Mile End Green, which extended south-east of this point. It was here, in 1381, that foot soldiers of the Peasants Revolt camped while the leaders met with 14-year-old Richard II. In July 1865, William Booth, founder of the Salvation Army, pitched his tent here and began preaching a message of hope to the poor of the East End. A statue of Booth and his wife Catherine stands upon the Waste.

The Waste was also an unregulated open-air market that had stood for hundreds of years and still exists today, though it's now licensed and is better known as the Whitechapel Market. It is situated between Vallance Road and Cambridge Heath Road. The market, once almost exclusively dominated by Jewish stallholders by the late nineteenth century, is mainly Bangladeshi-owned today, and stalls sell fabrics, jewellery and electrical goods. There was once a tollgate here, exactly 1 mile from the east City portal, Aldgate.

The Waste became a focal point in the East End for dissent and debate. The Social Democratic Federation held open-air meetings here in the late 1880s. Theodor Herzl, the father of Zionism, addressed a gathering here in 1898 and later the Jewish Tailors during their 1912 strike. The German anarchist Rudolf Rocker *(page 46)* also spoke at the same event.

***2* The Great Assembly Hall** The philanthropist, temperance campaigner and heir to the Charrington Brewery Frederick Charrington was so shocked by the misery that alcohol and vice were bringing to the working people of the East End, that he began a campaign to alleviate their suffering (he also declined his inheritance). As part of his endeavours he helped raise funds for the construction of a huge meeting hall, to be built by the Mile End Waste. The Great Assembly Hall, which opened in 1886, could hold over 5,000 people and on each Sunday thousands of impoverished East Enders would gather for tea, sustenance and religious worship. The building also contained meeting rooms and a bookshop. The Hall was also used as a rallying place for many trade unions in the throes of industrial disputes. The dockers involved in the Great Dock Strike of 1889 assembled here to hear their union leader, Ben Tillson, speak. In 1912, the Jewish Tailors strike against the 'sweated system' met here to discuss tactics. Included among the many speakers at the hall was Rudolph Rocker *(page 46)*. The hall was destroyed by a bomb in 1941 and has been replaced by the Tower Hamlets Mission.

**3 Fish and chips** It is recorded that an immigrant Jew, Joseph Malin, began selling fish and chips at 78 Cleveland Way around 1860 (78 Cleveland Way no longer exists and is covered by a paved area to the north of Cephas Street). Battered fish, that is fish prepared in the 'Jewish fashion', had arrived in Britain with the Sephardic (Spanish and Portuguese) Jews in the mid-seventeenth century. The Huguenots had almost certainly introduced fried slices of potatoes prepared in the 'French way' (French fries) to the East End, when they began to arrive in the late seventeenth century. Charles Dickens refers to fried potatoes in his 1859 novel, *A Tale of Two Cities* '*Husky chips of potatoes, fried with some reluctant drops of oil*'. However, there are some who claim that this early example of fusion food first appeared in Oldham, Lancashire.

**4 Wickhams and the Spiegelhalter resistance** A quick glance at the facia of what was once a grandiose department store on Mile End Road reveals a gap-toothed appearance. In the 1880s, a modest family-owned drapers store sat on the corner of Mile End Road and Cleveland Way. By the late 1920s, Wickhams had big plans to expand along the Mile End Road. However, standing in their way was a jewellers, Spiegelhalter at number 81. The Spiegelhalter's had moved from Germany to the East End in the late 1820s and, having already moved shop for Wickhams' expansion in the 1880s, they now refused to move again. So the department store, nicknamed the 'Harrods of the East', was built around the jewellery shop. The ionic sandstone columns simply never looked quite so grand with a section missing. Wickhams finally closed in the 1960s but Spiegelhalter continued trading until 1988. The building, now known as Dept W, has been split into multiple uses, but the 'gap' remains.



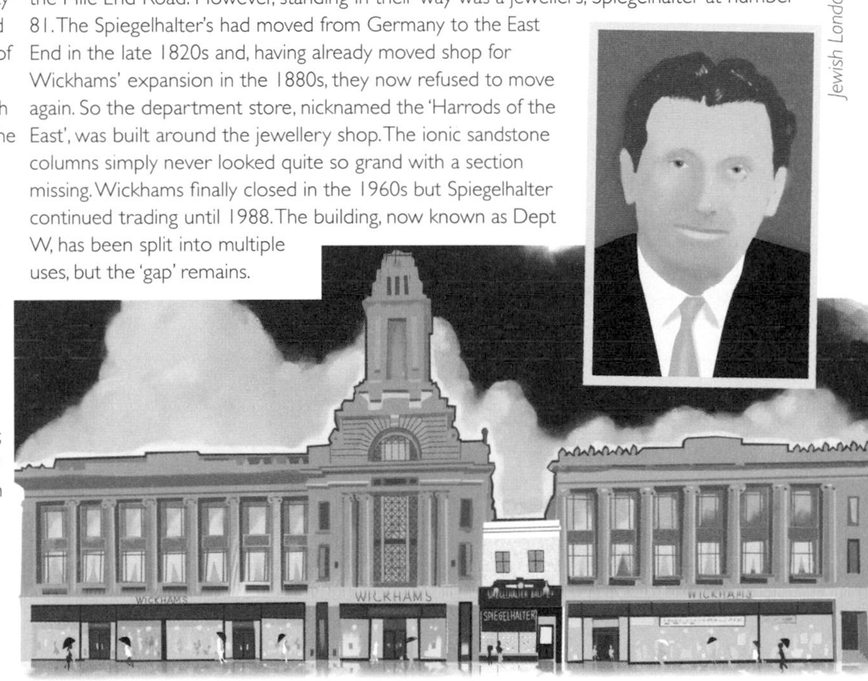


Cleveland Way

Stepney Green Underground

*Clockwise from top left: a map of Mile End Old Town (now Mile End Road), circa 1830 (note: Assembly Row); early fusion food – fish and chips; Barnet Winogradsky (later Lord Delfont), the Wickhams department store with the Spiegelhalter 'intrusion' as it appeared in the 1950s.*

**5 Paragon Theatre of Varieties** The young Charlie Chaplin appeared at the Paragon Theatre and was billed as a 'Hebrew' comic, presumably to attract Jewish customers. Despite rumours, there is no evidence that he was born of Jewish parents. The young Barnet Winogradsky, 1909–1994 *(above)*, later Lord Delfont, also appeared at the Paragon as a music hall performer before later becoming a successful theatre impresario. The theatre was demolished and a cinema now sits upon the site.

N

*Walking these pages 1.1km*

# EAST END

*Total walking distance 3.9km*

The Jewish populace of the East End increased exponentially following the Tzarist pogroms in 1881. Facilities such as bakeries, hostels, social clubs, theatres, cafés and a hospital were established to meet their kosher requirements. Within this world anarchists plotted, anti-fascists battled with Blackshirts and a supermarket chain was born.

***1* London Jewish Hospital** For many East End Jewish people, and especially the new arrivals from Eastern Europe after 1881, the kosher provisions at the London Hospital *(page 43)* were not sufficient. A campaign was started by a Polish-born barber, Isadore Berliner, to establish a medical facility where Yiddish language and customs would be the norm. Not all Jewish people accepted the proposed hospital, as some believed it would only encourage the use of Yiddish when they, as a community, should integrate into British society.

However, Berliner and his campaign team began collecting weekly penny donations and in 1916 work began on the site in Beaumont Square, despite the ongoing war. The voluntary out-patients facility of the London Jewish Hospital finally opened in 1919 with the medical wards, of 92 beds, opening two-years later.

In 1948, the hospital became part of the NHS and finally, in 1979, the property was sold for redevelopment, demolished and rebuilt as a private hospital.

***2* Rinkoff Bakery** Hyman Rinkoff arrived in the East End from Ukraine in 1911 and established a Jewish bakery. One hundred and ten years later it is still a family-run business and has outlets both in O'Leary Square and nearby, at 79 Vallance Road. The bakery is famous for its speciality breads and cakes, especially its challah and sourdough breads.

***3* Jubilee Street Club** The Jubilee Street Club was founded in 1906, by a group of Jewish anarchists led by a gentile, Rudolf Rocker. Rocker was a German-born Catholic who had been politically active in his homeland before arriving in London in 1895. He was on the run from German authorities due to his political stance. Rocker became the editor of several radical newspapers in London, including the Yiddish *Arbeter Fraynd* (Worker's Friend).

The club, at 165 Jubilee Street, was once a Methodist chapel that could hold 800 people. Lenin spoke here in 1903, at an event to mark the 32nd anniversary of the Paris Commune. The area was alive with anarchists and revolutionaries: Lenin returned to the area four years later along with Stalin, Gorky and Trotsky for the Congress of the Russian Social Democratic Labour Party *(page 42)*.

The Club was also a community centre for east European Jewish refugees (the street had a Jewish occupancy rate of between 50 and 75 per cent), but it also gave shelter to many fanatical anarchists. Among these were a Latvian gang, several members of whom were Jewish. They met here prior to their botched robbery of a jewellers in Houndsditch in late 1910, in which three policemen were killed.

In April 1912, the Jewish tailors of the West End went on strike for better pay. Their employers then switched much of their bespoke work to the East End sweatshops. By May, and influenced by *Arbeter Fraynd*, the tailors of the East End came out in solidarity with their West End counterparts. Rocker became a member of the strike committee and gave many inspirational speeches at gatherings at the Jubilee Club. Rocker asked the strikers to hold out against their employers, which they did, winning all their demands by the end of the month.

In 1914, Rocker published his anti-war opinions on the conflict that was raging

TESCO

TESCO

across Europe. As a result and being German, he was interned and the Anarchists club shut down. The building later became the Zionist Great Synagogue before being demolished to make way for housing.

**4 The Sidney Street Siege** During a jewellery heist in Houndsditch in December 1910, three unarmed policemen and the Latvian gang leader, George Gardstein, were killed. Those surviving members of the gang went into hiding and a major police manhunt began.

On 3 January 1911, following a tip-off that two members of the gang, Svaars and Sokoloff, were in hiding at 100 Sidney Street, the police immediately surrounded the house. Once the Latvians became aware of the police, they opened fire on them. The police responded with firearms that were no match for the gangsters' automatic weapons, so a detachment of Scots Guards was called up. The battle had now been raging for four hours and by midday, the home secretary, Winston Churchill, arrived to witness proceedings. One hour later flames were seen coming from the house, at which point Svaars put his head out of the window and was immediately shot by a marksman. Once the flames were doused, the bodies of Svaars and Sokoloff were recovered. A fireman was injured as a wall collapsed and later died. A small red plaque marks the location of 100 Sidney Street.

**5 Jack Cohen** The founder of the Tesco supermarket chain, Jack Cohen was born in nearby Walden Street in 1898. Cohen was the son of a Polish tailor and spent much of his childhood at 91 Ashfield Street. A plaque marks the house. After serving in the Royal Flying Corps during the First World War, he invested his demob money into purchasing surplus NAAFI stock, which he then resold on the market at Hackney, and the enterprise soon grew into a wholesale business.

The company name, Tesco, was derived from the initials of one of Cohen's business partner's, T E Stockwell, and the first two letters of Cohen's surname. The first two Tesco stores opened in 1931, in outer London. Following the Second World War, Cohen opened the first self-service supermarket in Britain, and the chain went on to become one of the largest in the country.

BAKERY

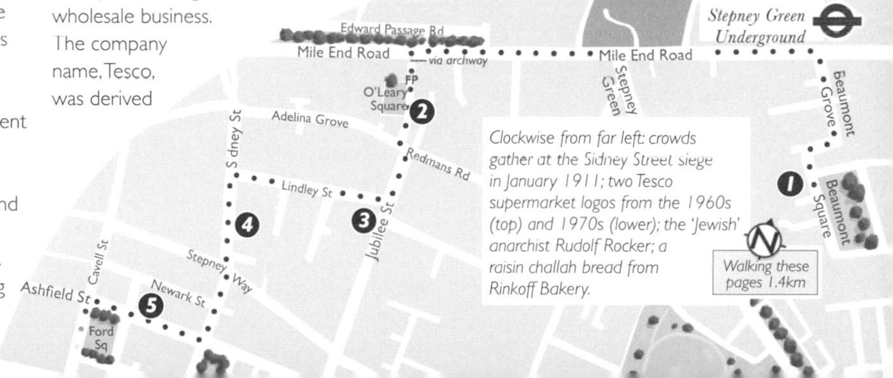

Edward Passage Rd
Mile End Road
via archway
Mile End Road
Stepney Green Underground
FP
O'Leary Square
Stepney Green
Beaumont Grove
Adelina Grove
Sidney St
Redmans Rd
Lindley St
Jubilee St
Beaumont Square
Stepney Way
Cavell St
Newark St
Ashfield St
Ford Sq
1 2 3 4 5
N
Walking these pages 1.4km

*Clockwise from far left: crowds gather at the Sidney Street siege in January 1911; two Tesco supermarket logos from the 1960s (top) and 1970s (lower); the 'Jewish' anarchist Rudolf Rocker; a raisin challah bread from Rinkoff Bakery.*

***1* The Grand Palais Theatre** In 1935, a Yiddish theatre, The Pavilion on Whitechapel Road, closed its doors for the last time *(page 42)*. In the same year, the Grand Palais Theatre opened at 133 Commercial Road with a plan to continue to cater for a Yiddish audience. The theatre had once been home to the Imperial Picture Palace.

The Palais became best known for its production of the *King of Lampedusa* in 1944. This was an anti-Nazi play based on a true story, written by Samuel Harendorf, concerning a Jewish RAF flight-sergeant, Sidney Cohen, who made a forced landing on the tiny Italian island of Lampedusa. The Italian garrison then surrendered to him, which earned Cohen the nickname 'The King of Lampedusa'. The play became a huge hit and even attracted a large non-Jewish audience.

The theatre remained open until 1970 and though the building still stands and its usage has changed, the original ornamental lintel is still in place above the main doors.

***2* The Berner Street Club** A tragic incident in 1888 brought this small, dingy office and courtyard located on Berner Street (now Henriques Street) to international infamy. It was home to a Jewish Men's Education Club, better known as the Berner Street Club, and was not so different to the one that would later be established on Jubilee Street *(page 46)*. The premises were very shabby, with bare wooden floors, drab furniture and a few portraits of Marx, Proudhon and Fenians lining the walls. It was a meeting place for largely Jewish tailors who came in search of entertainment and political discussion. The designer and socialist William Morris came here to read poetry. In 1885, the radical socialist newspaper *Arbeter Fraynd* (Worker's Friend) was founded here by Morris Winchevsky. The paper was also edited and printed on-site, although it struggled for funding and several times production had to cease.

*Clockwise from far left: A Grand Palais Theatre poster announcing performances of* The King of Lampedusa*; a detail of the Battle of Cable Street mural; a Salmon & Gluckstein cigarette container.*

In the early hours of 30 September 1888, the body of Elizabeth Stride was discovered in the courtyard of the club by a Jewish trader returning from a day's work. Stride's neck had been slashed: she had become

Jack the Ripper's third victim. The club closed in 1892, and the property was later demolished and replaced by a school.

**3 Salmon & Gluckstein tobacco factory** In the middle of the nineteenth century, German and Dutch Jews in London outnumbered Polish Jews by three to one (this would later change after the 1881 Tzarist pogroms). One of the main sources of trade for the former group was tobacco.

Samuel Gluckstein arrived in London from Germany in the early 1840s at the age of 20, and began working in a cigar factory in Soho. Over the next 20 years Gluckstein established his own business and moved the operation to 43 Leman Street, to be closer to the docks of London.

In 1873, Samuel's son, Monty Gluckstein, and his brother-in-law Barnett Salmon established the company Salmon & Gluckstein and by the start of the twentieth century had created a chain of 140 tobacconists. In 1902, Imperial Tobacco bought the company. Monty Gluckstein would later go on to found a chain of teashops with his brother-in-law Sir Joseph Lyon.

**4 Poor Jews Temporary Shelter** Simon Cohen, a baker, founded a shelter in the 1880s for Jewish people fleeing the Tzarist pogroms. Initially he housed the immigrants within his bakery, but this soon became unsanitary and unsatisfactory. In 1885, permanent lodgings were found at 84 Leman Street. Once at the shelter, the emigres could only reside for 14 days before moving on other accommodation, a job or the USA.

The shelter was partially funded by the Rothschild family. They encouraged those newly arrived to move on to the USA in a bid to decrease the amount of anti-Semitic feeling growing within the country.

**5 The Battle of Cable Street** During the 1930s, as the economy went into decline so fascism grew. While Hitler rose to power in Germany, Oswald Mosley formed the British Union of Fascists (BUF) in 1932. At a basic level the British fascists believed that most 'immigrants', including Jewish people, were stealing their jobs. The BUF organised numerous rallies mimicking those taking place in Nazi Germany.

One such rally was planned to occur in Victoria Park, Hackney on 4 October 1936, with a provocative march from Tower Hill going through the Jewish East End to the park. Mosley and around 4,000 fascists headed along Cable Street escorted by 6,000 policemen. It was known that the marchers would be resisted by thousands of dockers, socialists, anarchists and Jewish residents of the area. There banner and watchword was 'They shall not pass'. A petition had been presented to Parliament to ban the march but was rejected.

The marchers had only got as far as the intersection between Cable and Leman Street when they encountered resistance of a barricade constructed of an overturned truck, carts and timber. By now an estimated 100,000 anti-fascists had gathered in the area and when the police tried to clear the way for Oswald's Blackshirts, they were pelted with bricks and bottles. A running battle broke out between the two sides, with 90 people being arrested. Meanwhile, Mosley and his followers were forced to retreat westward along the Embankment and disperse. The East End witnessed much celebrating that evening.

For the Jewish community of the East End they sensed that it was now time to move on and, by 1939, many had relocated to the suburbs of London. A mural was painted on the wall of St George's Town Hall (**5b**) in 1983 by Dave Binnington, to commemorate the Battle of Cable Street.

# WEST END

*Total walking distance 3.5km*

This walk through a very well-heeled district of central London, reveals several residences of wealthy and philanthropic families, the home of the only Jewish-born prime minister and how the flashing amber light pedestrian crossing came to be named.

**1 West London Synagogue** In 1840, a group of Jewish people living in the West End began a reform movement. Having moved away from Spitalfields and Whitechapel, they did not wish to walk a ten-mile round journey to the East End every Sabbath to attend synagogue. They wanted services with more decorum and in English and they wanted to unite the Ashkenazi and Sephardic assemblies. It became known as the Reform movement, and their first breakaway synagogue was built in Burton Street, St Pancras.

Soon this synagogue was too small to accommodate the growing congregation and so they moved, first to Margaret Street and finally, in 1870, to 34 Upper Berkley Street. The annual membership fee, of £7 (about £850 today), indicated that this was an exclusive synagogue only for the wealthy of the district.

The Byzantine-inspired interior of the synagogue features marble columns supporting the gallery and a central dome. It is the only British synagogue with an installed pipe organ.

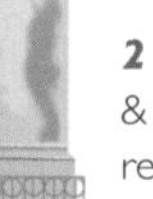

**2 Marks & Spencer** Marks & Spencer is a major British retailer with its flagship store located on Oxford Street, close to Marble Arch. The company was founded in 1894 by a Polish-born Jew, Michael Marks, and Yorkshire-born bookkeeper, Thomas Spencer. Together they established a penny bazaar in the Leeds Kirkgate covered market. It became so successful that they founded more outlets across the north of England and beyond. Today, the company has around 1,500 stores in the UK and abroad.

**3 Moses Montefiore** Following his retirement at the age of 40, Sir Moses Montefiore moved into the house at 99 Park Lane, which became his home for the next 60 years. Born in 1784, Montefiore became a celebrated person within the world of British Jewry. He began his working life trading in wholesale tea and groceries, then progressed to become a stockbroker. In 1806, following a calamitous investment in a fraudulent scheme, he lost all his clients' money, and had to step down as a broker.

Within ten years Montefiore was back trading on the Royal Exchange *(page 29)*, where he made a fortune investing in a gas street lighting venture and establishing the Alliance Assurance Company. Such was the financial return that he could afford to take early retirement. He married Judith Cohen, whose sister was married to Nathan Mayer Rothschild.

Montefiore then devoted himself and his wealth to philanthropic causes both in the UK and abroad. He travelled widely often to assist oppressed Jewish people in Europe and the Middle East. He developed education, work and health schemes for the Jewish communities in Palestine, and encouraged them to move to these developments. Montefiore could be seen as an early Zionist.

In 1835, he became president of the Jewish Board of Deputies; a position he would hold for 50 years. Two years later, following a change in legislation, he was permitted, as a Jew, to become the

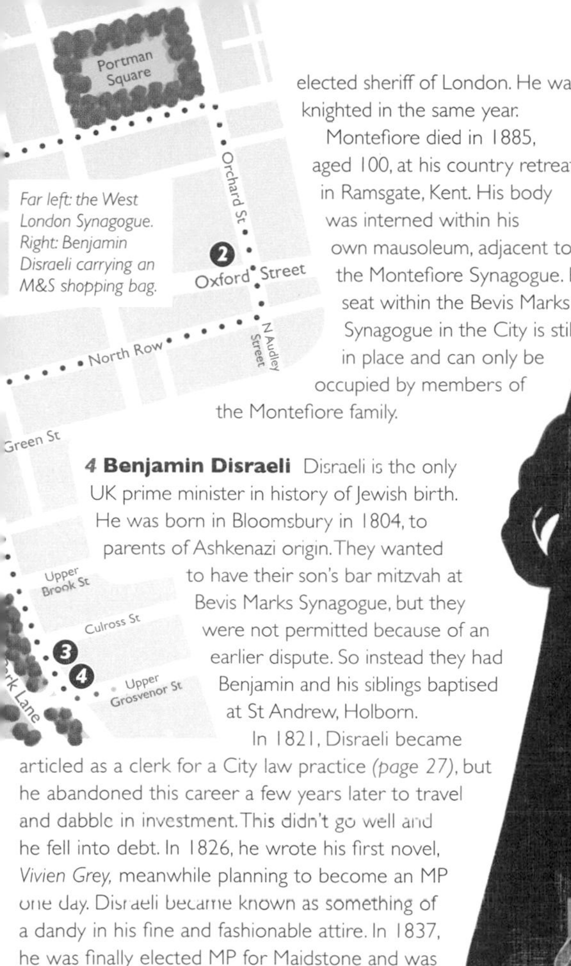


*Far left: the West London Synagogue. Right: Benjamin Disraeli carrying an M&S shopping bag.*

elected sheriff of London. He was knighted in the same year.

Montefiore died in 1885, aged 100, at his country retreat in Ramsgate, Kent. His body was interned within his own mausoleum, adjacent to the Montefiore Synagogue. His seat within the Bevis Marks Synagogue in the City is still in place and can only be occupied by members of the Montefiore family.

**4 Benjamin Disraeli** Disraeli is the only UK prime minister in history of Jewish birth. He was born in Bloomsbury in 1804, to parents of Ashkenazi origin. They wanted to have their son's bar mitzvah at Bevis Marks Synagogue, but they were not permitted because of an earlier dispute. So instead they had Benjamin and his siblings baptised at St Andrew, Holborn.

In 1821, Disraeli became articled as a clerk for a City law practice *(page 27)*, but he abandoned this career a few years later to travel and dabble in investment. This didn't go well and he fell into debt. In 1826, he wrote his first novel, *Vivien Grey,* meanwhile planning to become an MP one day. Disraeli became known as something of a dandy in his fine and fashionable attire. In 1837, he was finally elected MP for Maidstone and was able, as a Christian, to take the oath of office. The Jewish MP Lionel de Rothschild, elected in 1847, was unable to take the same oath and therefore prevented from taking his seat. It would be another 11 years before Rothschild could become an active MP. Disraeli spoke in favour of amending the law.

In 1839, Disraeli married Mary Anne Lewis, wife of the late Wyndham Lewis, a backer of his election campaign. Disraeli and Mary moved into 93 Park Lane, becoming neighbours with Moses Montefiore (**3**).

After over 30 years in politics, Disraeli was elected leader of the Conservative party and, in 1868, he became prime minister for 11 months. In his second term of office, beginning in 1874, his government introduced several radical reforms that enabled better public housing, health and education. In 1875, due to Disraeli's collaboration with Lionel de Rothschild, the British government became a major share-holder in the Suez Canal, a strategic maritime waterway for British interests. The following year Disraeli was ennobled as 1st Earl of Beaconsfield and was elevated to the Lords. Following the government's defeat at the polls in 1880, Disraeli moved into 19 Curzon Street just off Park Lane, his wife having died eight years earlier. In 1881, he contracted bronchitis and died later that year.

N

*Walking these pages 1.6km*

**1 Belisha beacon** The ubiquitous flashing amber Belisha beacon was introduced by Leslie Hore-Belisha to the roads of Britain in the 1930s. Hore-Belisha was born to a Jewish family in 1893. Following his service during the First World War, Hore-Belisha returned to Oxford and qualified as a barrister. In 1923, he entered Parliament as a Liberal MP and gained a reputation as a magnificent speaker.

He was appointed Minister of Transport in 1934, during the period of National Government. Speed limits for motor vehicles did not exist in the early 1930s, so in the Road Traffic Act of 1934, a 30mph limit was introduced in built-up areas. Hore-Belisha also oversaw the rewriting of the Highway Code and the introduction of a driving test for all drivers. It was his introduction of the pedestrian crossing with flashing amber beacons that enabled his name live on.

Prior to the Second World War, Hore-Belisha was promoted to Secretary of State for War. However, he was dismissed from the post in 1940, possibly as a result of military anti-Semitism.

**2 Alfred de Rothschild** Alfred de Rothschild was born in 1842, the second son of Lionel and Charlotte de Rothschild. At the age of 21, Alfred, having failed to get a degree at Cambridge, was employed in the family firm of N M Rothschild Bank, and it was here that he gained experience of banking and the financial world, so much so that five years later he became the first Jewish director of the Bank of England, a post he held for 21 years.

Throughout his life, de Rothschild was a serious art collector. Following one expensive purchase, a dealer claimed that he had made very little on the transaction. However, de Rothschild was able to access the art merchant's bank account and saw that this was not the case. Once the Bank of England discovered that he had been prying into a client's account, he was dismissed from his post.

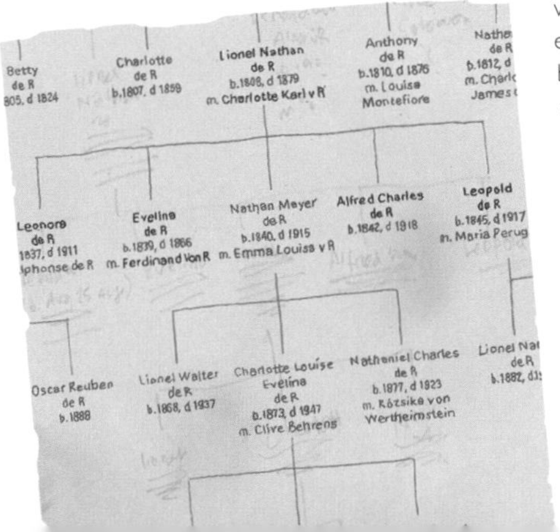

Rothschild later worked as a British diplomat, serving as a consul-general to Austria before the First World War. During the war he returned to N M Rothschild Bank. He lived at Seamore Place, with its imposing views of Hyde Park (the street has since been renamed Curzon Square and the house demolished). In 1879, de Rothschild inherited his father's country estate at Halton in Buckinghamshire. It was here and at Seamore Place that he would entertain many from the world of politics, entertainment and royalty, including Edward, Prince of Wales.

De Rothschild became a close friend of Disraeli *(page 51)*, who lived nearby at 19 Curzon Street. He died in 1918, after a short illness.

**3 Leopold de Rothschild** Leopold was born in 1845 to Lionel and Charlotte de Rothschild. Four years later, his father would become the first Jewish MP. In his early years, Leopold followed in his older brothers' footsteps by attending Cambridge and afterwards taking employment in the family business of N M Rothschild. Following the death of his uncle, Baron Mayer de Rothschild, Leopold became head of the banking operation.

Horse racing became a favourite pastime of Leopold's and he established a thoroughbred stud farm in Bedfordshire that would go on to produce many race winners. He inherited the property at 5 Hamilton Place following his father's death.

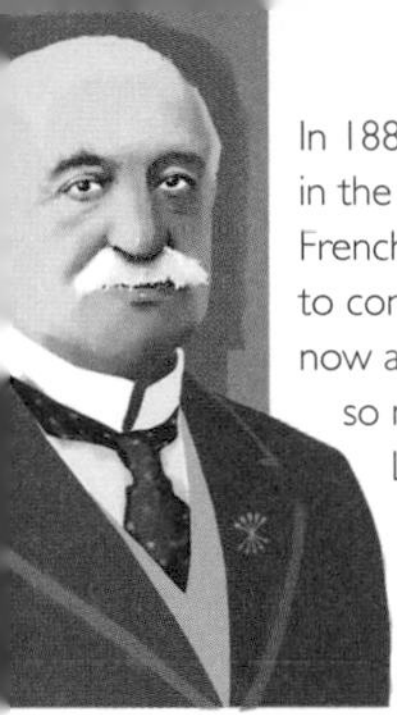

In 1881, he had the dwelling remodelled in the style of a fine seventeenth-century French house, the work taking two years to complete. The house still stands and is now a private club, Les Ambassadeurs. Like so many of the de Rothschild's family, Leopold undertook a lot of charitable work. He also became president of the United Synagogue and the Jews' Free School.

**4 Rothschild Row** Close to what is now the busy Piccadilly traffic gyratory system stood a row of very grand houses nicknamed 'Rothschild Row'. Of these fine edifices only Apsley House at 149 Piccadilly still remains. This address was once the residence of the general and prime minister, the Duke of Wellington.

Lionel and Charlotte de Rothschild acquired the property at 148 Piccadilly (then known as The Terrace) in 1845. Charlotte was expecting their fifth child, Leopold, to add to the existing family of Leonora, Evelina, Nathan Mayer and Alfred. Number 148 Piccadilly was described as one of the best addresses in London. However, not content with one already sizable house, Lionel bought number 147 in 1859 and had the two properties amalgamated. Earlier in 1825, Lionel's father, Nathan Mayer Rothschild *(page 28)*, acquired a house at 107 Piccadilly in 1825, which is now the site of the Sheraton Hotel.

The youngest daughter of Lionel and Charlotte de Rothschild, Evelina, married her second cousin Ferdinand von Rothschild. Ferdinand purchased number 143 Piccadilly in 1865 as the marital home. Sadly, Evelina died while giving birth the following year. Shortly afterwards Ferdinand's sister, Alice von Rothschild, acquired the property next door (number 142) so that she could be close to her widowed brother. By the 1950s, the properties had changed hands and eventually they were purchased and demolished to make way for the Piccadilly gyratory system, which opened in 1963.

**5 Holocaust Memorial Garden** The Holocaust Memorial is dedicated to the six million Jewish people murdered by the Nazis during the Second World War. It was created in 1983 and was funded by the Board of Deputies of British Jews. The largest of the boulders carries the inscription '*For these I weep. Streams of tears flow from my eyes because of the destruction of my people*' from the Book of Lamentations, inscribed in both English and Hebrew.

HOLOCAUST MEMORIAL GARDEN

Upper Grosvenor St
S Audley St
Reeve Mews
320m
Stanhope Gate
Curzon St
Curzon Sq
FP
Pitt's Head Mews
London Hilton
Hertford St
Park Lane
HYDE PARK
300m
Serpentine Rd
Old Park Lane
Hamilton Place
Piccadilly
Hyde Park Corner Underground

*Clockwise from far left: a pair of Belisha beacons; Leopold de Rothschild; the Holocaust Memorial stone in Hyde Park; a section of the de Rothschild family tree.*

*Walking these pages 1.9km*

# CHINESE LONDON

## The first Chinese person in Britain

In 1687, Shen Fu Tsung became the first-known Chinese person to visit Britain. Until the nineteenth century China was all but closed to the outside world with very few people allowed to leave or enter. Shen, who had travelled to Europe to become a Jesuit priest, met James II and other notable figures in England. The King was so moved by the meeting with Shen that he commissioned a portrait of him. After his Jesuit instruction, Shen sailed back to China in 1691, although he died en route.

**The Opium Wars** By the early nineteenth century the British East India Company (EIC) had a lucrative trade selling British goods to China in return for tea. The demand for tea became so excessive in Britain that the EIC started shipping opium from its own plantations in India to China via private traders. Opium smoking in China was on the increase and the EIC was feeding this addiction. The ships returning to Britain carried silks, ceramics and of course tea.

By 1838, Daoguang Emperor decided to cut the trade in opium that was killing so many of his people and so depleted the national reserves. The Chinese authorities then confiscated 1.5 million kilograms of opium. The British government viewed this as an attack on their trade and declared war. The British overcame the Chinese forces and imposed the Treaty of Nanking in 1842, which included Hong Kong becoming a British colony.

A second Opium War flared up in 1858, between the same adversaries. Britain, victors again, achieved even greater trading rights with China and, following the opening of the Suez Canal in 1869, commerce with the Far East increased. The number of Chinese sailors who began to arrive at British docks also increased.

**Limehouse** Once the ships arrived at the East India Docks in Blackwall, many of the international crews, including Chinese sailors, would take temporary shelter before the return journey home. This could be for several weeks. However, once their pay had expired, many were reduced to begging on the streets until their homebound ship departed.

A small community of Chinese people, mostly seamen, became established just to the west of the docks in Limehouse in the 1880s, and soon the district became known as Chinatown. The 1901 Census put the Chinese population of Limehouse at only 120, though this will have excluded many transient seamen and those living illegally in the area.

Some Chinese seamen simply decided to remain in the area, having reached an age when life on the waves was becoming too dangerous and tiring. Though they could not be legally employed, they found casual work in the few launderettes that were established in the area by those Chinese

sailors who had secured British citizenship.

Unlike many of the minority ethnic groups mentioned in this book, the Chinese people that came to Britain, usually through one of the major ports such as Liverpool, Cardiff or London, were not political or religious refugees but usually sailors who had decided to jump ship or simply stay in Britain, sometimes after striking up romantic relationships with local women.

By the beginning of the twentieth century, many British dockers and seamen began to see the Chinese workers as a threat to their livelihoods. In 1916, during the First World War, the Trades Union Congress motioned that all Chinese people be repatriated (even though many were assisting in the war effort). The government did not accept the proposal, although the Aliens Act of 1905 was beefed-up after the war with restrictions placed on Chinese merchant seamen. With this, the Great Depression and the reduction in shipping, the number of Chinese people living in Limehouse began to decline.

**Chinese laundry** Before the introduction of mechanised washing machines, laundry was very much an arduous, manual task. For those who could afford it, dirty clothes were sent out to private laundries. The need for such services

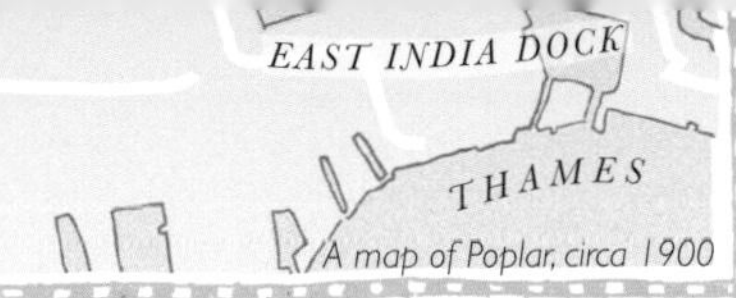

A map of Poplar, circa 1900

grew in the nineteenth century. Prejudice and the law forbade Chinese people from taking jobs in Britain, and so some took to setting up laundry services within Limehouse. The cost of setting up such an establishment was relatively inexpensive.

Often these Chinese laundries became an easy target for attacks by racist gangs. In 1901, dockers and sailors, afraid that the Chinese were undercutting rates of pay, stoned a newly opened laundry in Limehouse.

After the Second World War electric washing machines reduced the need for manual services. Those employed in the laundries then switched to establishing businesses in the catering industry.

**Limehouse portrayed** To pass the time while awaiting the next ship home, it was reported in the British press that many Chinese men would gamble, smoke opium and entrap white women. This was far from true, as most Chinese people were, like other immigrant groups, generally quiet and law abiding.

Until 1916, cocaine and other drugs were legally available in Britain. Regardless, the press and certain novelists wanted to paint a seedier side to life in Limehouse, with its 'sleazy opium and gambling dens'. Far more drugs were consumed at fashionable West End parties and more money squandered away on the roulette wheels, but this was not what the paying public wanted to hear.

Several novels published in the 1910s sought to portray Chinese people in a poor light. In Thomas Burke's *Limehouse Nights*, he wrote tales of 'opium-addled Chinese men', pursuing English women, while Sax Rohmer created *Dr Fu Manchu*: an evil Chinese mastermind planning to destroy Western civilisation.

The author Loa She lived in London between 1927 and 1929. Having observed how the British press were portraying his fellow countrymen, he commented:

*'If there were twenty Chinese living in Chinatown, their own account would say five thousand; moreover, everyone of these five thousand yellow devils would certainly smoke opium, smuggle arms, murder people then stuff the corpses under the bed, and rape women regardless of age'.*

**The Blitz** During the Second World War, German bombers helped complete what the urban planners had started in the late 1930s: the demolition of many slum houses in Limehouse. During one bombing raid in 1940, 70 Chinese seamen were killed in a Limehouse lodging house.

Such was the destruction to the East End of London during the war, only a few Chinese families remained in the area afterwards. By 1963, virtually all of the Limehouse slum dwellings had been bulldozed and replaced.

**To Soho** It is believed that the first time the British public at large experienced Chinese food was at the London International Health Exhibition of 1884. Among the displays was the first Chinese restaurant, with cuisine prepared by chefs from Beijing and Guangzhou. The first permanent Chinese restaurant opened near Piccadilly in the early 1900s. The rents in nearby Soho were cheap and the first Gerrard Street Chinese restaurant opened soon after. The growth of Chinese eateries in Britain was exponential. In 1957, there were 50 restaurants; by 1966, there were over 1,000. This was mainly due to a large number of Chinese immigrants arriving from Hong Kong. Also, many British servicemen returning from the Far East after the Second World War wanted to rediscover the cuisine, although many menu items were heavily anglicised and sometimes served with chips. However, the big lure was that Chinese restaurants opened late, after pub closing hours and were affordable.

By 1970, Soho had a growing Chinese community of restaurants, hairdressers and a travel agency. Ten years later the list of restaurants and services had grown to around 100. And they were no longer catering only for a local Chinese population but for tourists and theatregoers flocking to the West End.

From a few hundred Chinese seamen and dockers establishing laundries and small restaurants in Limehouse, today the area has grown into the vibrant Chinatown of Soho.

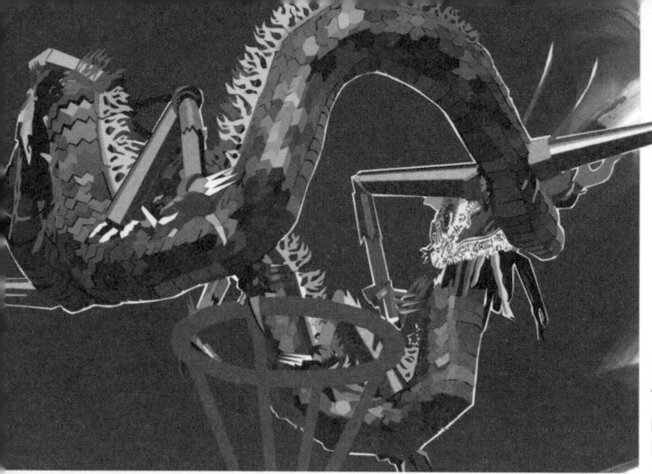

# LIMEHOUSE

*Total walking distance 1.4km*

From the 1860s onwards, some Chinese sailors, rather than return to sea, began to settle in Limehouse and although the area was not exclusively Chinese, the sight and smells of their shops, cafés and the occasional opium den gave it a unique atmosphere that earned it the name 'Chinatown'. Very few of the buildings described in this chapter survived the Blitz or the slum clearance.

***1* Limehouse Causeway** The first Cantonese sailors began taking residence in Limehouse Causeway around the 1860s. The housing stock was old and the rents cheap, but it was also close to their main source of work in the East India Dock. Limehouse Causeway was then a much narrower street than its present-day counterpart. In 1934, the street was widened and nearly all of the existing property demolished. Several opium dens existed here, including one at 24 Limehouse Causeway belonging to the husband of Ada Ping You. Ping You gained notoriety and was imprisoned for supplying opium and cocaine to the actor Billie Carleton in November 1918. Soon after, Carleton died of a drug overdose. This story, though very much a one-off incident, further fuelled the appetite of the public for salacious novels by Sax Rohmer and Thomas Burke, set in the world of Limehouse opium dens.

**2 Dr Philip William Lamb** Ping Win Lam was born in Hong Kong in 1893, the second eldest of five sons. Lam received a good education and learned English at Queens College, Hong Kong. By the age of 17 and encouraged by his father, he was despatched to Edinburgh University to begin his medical training. In 1917, during the First World War, he qualified as a doctor and began his medical probation at Leicester Royal Infirmary and the nearby military hospital. It would all be good preparation for what he would experience 20 years later.

In 1920, Lam established his first practice at 63 East India Dock Road, Limehouse (*location* **2,** *next page*) to work with the local Chinese and other residents of the community. He also worked as a clinical assistant in the Royal Westminster Ophthalmic Hospital. It was at this time that he decided to anglicise his name to Philip William Lamb. Dr Lamb *(right)* had a strong social conscience and would often provide medical care free of charge if he knew his patients could not afford to pay for treatment. Upon his death in 1981, the *Sing Tao* newspaper would write in Dr Lamb's obituary '... *he treated poor students and compatriots, with no fees, benefitting many Chinese expatriates*'.

In 1927, Lamb had moved his practice to 82 West India Dock Road. His patients were mainly Shanghai Chinese people who lived in the Pennyfields area. In the

same year he made Hampstead Garden Suburb, close to Golders Green, north London, his home until 1935. After the surgery took a direct hit in 1940, during the Blitz, he moved into the building a few doors up and continued to work as a doctor until 1968. During the Blitz, Dr Lamb would go from shelter to shelter to treat the injured, regardless of risk to himself.

The National Health Service was established in 1948, however Dr Lamb, despite his altruistic tendencies, continued with his private practice in Harley Street and his surgery in Limehouse. He had many Chinese patients who would travel across the globe to be treated by him.

He and his Scottish wife, whom he married in 1939, continued to live in Golders Green, and he died here, at the age of 87. Lamb was a very well-respected doctor not only within Limehouse but also among the various ambassadors and staff of Chinese Embassy, both before and after the Communist Revolution of 1949.

**3 The first Chinese takeaway** In the late 1960s, Charlie Cheung owned several popular Chinese restaurants in and around Limehouse. His Old Friends restaurant was located on the corner of West India Dock Road and Mandarin Street (the latter street no longer exists). One of his other outlets, Local Friends, at 102 Salmon Lane (approx. 600m away), claimed to be the first dedicated Chinese takeaway in the UK.

**4 The Dragons' Gate** These two chasing dragons, Chinese symbols of good fortune and fertility, were commissioned in 1996. They are located here to celebrate the Chinese community that once lived and worked in Limehouse.

**5 The Strangers' Home** By the 1850s, Chinese seamen begging on the streets of the East End was becoming a common sight. In many instances they had been abandoned by their captain or shipping company. The Royal Victoria Dock had opened in 1855, making London one of the largest import-export docks in the world. The problem of forsaken foreign sailors was becoming more acute. At this time, many merchant vessels were still wind powered. Long-distance vessels were dependent on the trade winds thus often delaying return journeys to the Far East. As a response to this increasing problem, a hostel called the Strangers' Home was established in 1857, on West India Dock Road. It was paid for by various East End Christian missionary groups and the East India Company. The refuge could accommodate 220 seamen who were penniless and awaiting a home-bound ship. However, some sailors, who had just had enough of sailing or were now too old for the sea, decided to try and make a living in Limehouse. West India House now occupies the site that the Strangers' Home once stood upon.

*Clockwise from top left: the Dragons' Gate, built as a memorial to the first Chinatown in London; the Strangers' Home, next to the Ships Chandlers (still standing); Dr Philip William Lamb in 1917.*

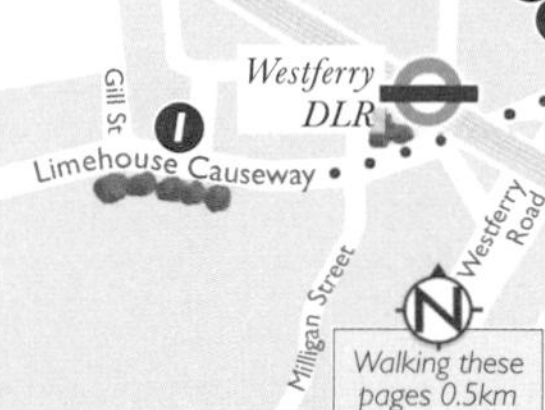

**1 Amoy Place** Amoy Place and nearby Pennyfields became the location where sailors from the region of Shanghai chose to congregate and often settled. Those newly arrived often lacked the ability to speak English, and this combined with prejudice against immigrants meant that they could were unable to take regular employment. A few enterprising Chinese people established laundries in Amoy Place, where the rents were cheap and they could provide a service to the locals of Poplar while employing fellow countrymen. Amoy Place was badly damaged during the Blitz.

**2 Surgery** This is the site of Dr Philip William Lamb's first Limehouse surgery *(page 56)*.

**3 Pennyfields** The 1881 Census Report revealed that 37 Irish dockers and labourers lived in Pennyfields. However, within 20 years Chinese people had begun to occupy more houses and the name 'Chinatown' was being applied to the Pennyfields and Limehouse Causeway areas. By 1918, the number of registered Chinese inhabitants in Pennyfields was over 180. Despite the housing stock in Pennyfields being dilapidated, several press stories reported that the interior of the Chinese abodes, businesses and shops were well maintained and clean. Charles Booth's Poverty Map of 1889 also concurred with this description.

The Chung Hwa School was established on Pennyfields in 1928, to teach children born to Chinese people in the area about their culture and language. Irene Ho, daughter of Sir Robert Ho Tung, a Hong Kong businessman and philanthropist (and friend of Dr Lamb, *page 56*), founded the school.

**4 Blockaded** The first Chinese laundry opened on Pennyfields in 1901, and it was almost immediately stoned by an angry mob. It may have been seen as a representation of Chinese expansion into the area and the undercutting of British seamen and dockworkers' pay. Seven years later British seamen blockaded the Board of Trade Mercantile Marine office on East India Dock Road. Fights broke out and the police had to intervene. Unusually for the area the building has neither been bombed nor demolished.

*Clockwise from above right: a Chinese cobblers on Pennyfields c.1920; the Chinese Embassy on Portland Place; a ghost street sign on Amoy Place.*

# WEST END

*Total walking distance 2.6km*

This walk is through London's West End, taking you from the Chinese Embassy into the very heart of new Chinatown and its array of restaurants.

**1 The Cultural Revolution (in London)** During the Chinese Cultural Revolution, the authorities in Hong Kong closed a Communist newspaper and 'charged journalists with inciting violence. As a consequence the Red Guard set fire to the British Embassy in Peking on 22 August 1967. The staff and guests were attacked and the building destroyed. Meanwhile in London, Special Branch officers were posted to watch the Chinese Embassy at 51 Portland Place. A week later, as a member of the Chinese Embassy staff was returning from a meeting at the Foreign Office, around 20 staff burst out of the Embassy and attacked police with axes, batons and dustbin lids. Three policemen and a photographer sustained head injuries in the melee.

**2 Defector Kuo Teh-lou** Mr Kuo was a chef working at the Chinese Embassy. In 1963 he was encouraged by friends to defect and set up his own restaurant, Kuo Yuan, in Willesden High Road, north-west London. It was the first restaurant to serve Peking cuisine (including the now-ubiquitous Peking duck). Prior to this, most Chinese food in London was of the Cantonese variety. The Kuo Yuan was firmly placed on the gastronomic map after a visit from Princess Margaret and Lord Snowden.

**3 Kidnapped** As Dr Sun Yat Sen was walking along Portland Place in October 1896, two members of staff from the Chinese Legation approached him and forced him into the Embassy (which was then located at 47 Portland Place, in what is now the Polish Embassy). Dr Sun had fled China because of his revolutionary ambitions to overthrow the Manchu dynasty and had travelled to London via the USA. Now that he was held captive in the Embassy, Sun believed he would be smuggled back to China, interrogated and executed. Sun managed to bribe a British servant within the Embassy to take a message to a Dr Cantlie, his former medical tutor, stating that he was being held hostage. Initially the police and press wouldn't believe Cantlie, so he approached the Foreign Office. They placed the Embassy under surveillance to prevent Sun being smuggled out of the country. Finally 12 days after he was kidnapped, a British newspaper, *The Globe*, took notice and published the story. This was now becoming a diplomatic incident and the British government demanded that the Chinese Embassy release Sun, which they promptly did, though claiming that he had entered the Embassy voluntarily.

Dr Sun went on to travel the globe and spread his ideas of revolutionary change within China. In 1911, his ambition finally became reality when the first Republic of China was established and Sun was elected its first president.

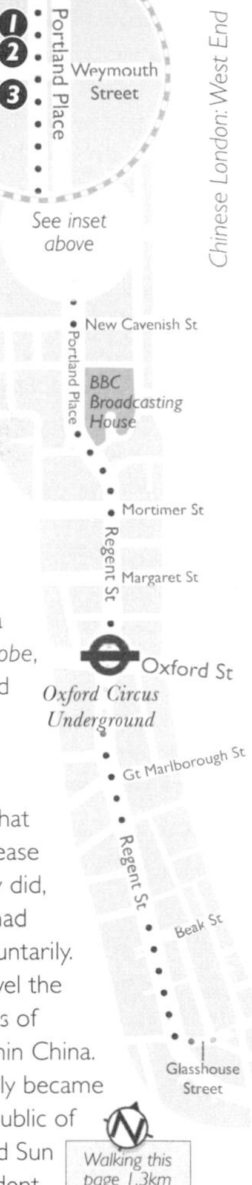

**1 Early West End restaurants** The first time the British public sampled Chinese food was at the 1884 International Health Exhibition in London. However, another 24 years would lapse before the first Chinese restaurants opened in the West End. The first establishment, on Piccadilly, was unsurprisingly called The Chinese, this was followed by The Cathay which opened on Glasshouse Street and later Maxims in Soho.

These Chinese restaurants offered traditional Cantonese fare of meats and fish 'lacquered' in oyster sauce and served at affordable prices. However, often lacking traditional Chinese ingredients, the chefs created several new dishes for Western palates including chop suey and sweet and sour pork.

Chop suey was not a truly authentic Chinese dish but is believed to have been created in America in the late nineteenth century, by Chinese migrants, with the recipe, a stir-fried combination of meat, usually chicken or pork, with vegetables and bean sprouts in a thick sauce, being imported to London.

**2 Ley-On's Restaurant** Ley-On was born in Canton in 1890, migrated to London and, by 1926, he had become one of the first Chinese restaurateurs to open an establishment in Gerrard Street, Soho (**2a**). He had previously owned a restaurant in Limehouse catering mainly for Chinese seamen. Within six years Ley-On had moved his Soho restaurant twice before settling at 89–91 Wardour Street (**2b**). Ley-On furnished the restaurant in a lavish Chinese style and it became a focal point for Chinese society to meet. Although a successful restaurateur, Ley-On always had ambitions to be a film actor. He played the parts of minor Chinese characters in eight films, such as the 1950s *Black Rose* (which starred Orson Welles). He even played an Inuit in the wartime film *49th Parallel*. Many of his actor colleagues would frequent Ley-On's restaurant.

During the 1948 London Olympic Games it was Ley-On who supplied the chefs for the Chinese team. Ley-On's Chop Suey Restaurant also catered for a local audience and served quite an extensive British menu. Chinese menus were often long and full of 'exotic' ingredients. Another nearby Chinese restaurant, Poon's in Lisle Street, introduced the first set menu, as the owner noticed how often the British clientele struggled to choose from hundreds of dishes.

**3 The Chinatown Gate** This ornamental gate of Qing Dynasty style was opened in 2016.

**4 Gerrard Street** Baron Gerard of Brandon, Suffolk, owned a sizable piece of land on what was formerly military training ground in Soho. In 1677, he commissioned the property developer Nicholas Barbon to lay out a new district of streets, which included one to be named after himself, Gerrard Street (the second 'r' was added later). This new zone, close to Westminster, became popular with the wealthy. An early resident was the poet John Dryden, who lived at 44 Gerrard Street from 1687. By the early eighteenth century Huguenot immigrants began to move into the area, especially those skilled in working precious metals *(page 18)*.

Over the centuries the maintenance of these properties declined (Charles Dickens makes reference to the area's decline in his novel 1861 *Great Expectations*: 'in want of painting, and with dirty windows'). By the early twentieth century many

buildings were so dilapidated that landlords offered cheap rent. The area soon became renowned for nightclubs and the sex trade. In 1959, the first Ronnie Scott's Jazz Club opened in the basement of 39 Gerrard Street. Several international restaurants, including Chinese, began to appear.

In 1975, the area was declared a conservation zone thus saving it from the bulldozer, and by the early 1980s it had earned the name 'Chinatown', owing to the increased number of Chinese restaurants that had begun to dominate both Gerrard and Lisle Street.

**5 The Nanking** Fung Saw, a prospective Labour candidate for the Holborn constituency, established The Nanking restaurant at 4 Denmark Street in 1934. Around that time several other Chinese and Japanese restaurants were located in the same street. The Nanking became a gathering place for political meetings, musicians and writers. The anti-imperialist Progressive Writers Association was established here in 1935. Denmark Street was also developing as a centre for music publication. Fung sold the restaurant in 1964 and it was converted into the Regent Sound Studio. It was here, in the same year, that the Rolling Stones recorded their self-titled debut album.

**Kenneth Lo** Lo was born in China in 1913 to wealthy parents, who six years later moved the family to London for his father to take up a post in the Chinese Embassy. Though educated in London, Lo returned to China to attend university and while there he honed his skills as a tennis player, eventually representing China in the Davis Cup. In 1936, he returned to Britain to study English literature at Cambridge.

Following in his father's footsteps, he became a Chinese consul in north-west England. Lo once settled a union dispute between Chinese and West Indian seaman in Liverpool with a feast of Chinese food.

A chance meeting with a publishing friend in 1954 resulted in him writing *Cooking the Chinese Way*, even though his only real knowledge of Chinese food was not cooking it but eating it. The book sold well, tapping into a new curiosity about Chinese food. Lo went on to write 40 cookery books and established two upmarket Chinese restaurants in London. He died in 1995.

*Clockwise from left: a 1950s menu from Ley-On's restaurant; Kenneth Lo; The Chinatown Gate in Wardour Street.*

# BLACK LONDON

In his book *Staying Power*, Peter Fryer states *'There were people of Africa in Britain long before the English came'*. Around the year AD 253 there is evidence of black African soldiers on duty at Hadrian's Wall in Northumberland. Twelve hundred years later, during the brief reign of Mary I, it was recorded that a trader, John Lok, brought five African men to London in 1555. It is very possible that they were enslaved people. In 1562, John Hawkins captured 300 Guinean men, then shipped them to the Caribbean and sold them to the Spanish plantation owners of Hispaniola (now Haiti).

**The Triangular Trade** The process of enslaving African people and shipping them to the Americas proved to be very profitable for many white European enslavers. In 1454, Pope Nicholas V had given his papal blessing to Iberian monarchs to seek out 'pagans' and 'nonbelievers' and force them into a life of slavery. Ships laden with textiles, muskets, gunpowder and beer left Europe for the west coast of Africa. These items were traded for local Africans (young men, women and children), who were manacled and then shipped to the Americas. In some instances, Africans were captured by fellow Africans and sold to European enslavers. They were quite unaware of the horrors into which they were sending them.

Many thousands of enslaved people were overwhelmed by disease or the brutalities enacted by the ships' crews, did not survive the passage and were thrown overboard. Those enslaved people who survived the 'middle passage' to the New Worlds were then sold to plantation owners. The ships returned on the final leg back to Europe with cargoes of rum, sugar, tobacco and coffee. Life for the enslaved people was extremely harsh with around one in three dying during the first three years of 'existence' in the Americas as a result of suicide or disease. It is believed that at least 12 million slaves were transported across the Atlantic to the Americas.

**London slavery** The trading of enslaved people was immensely lucrative in the eighteenth century. Numerous well-known banks, including Barings and Barclays, invested heavily in this commerce. One director of the Bank of England owned six slave ships along with numerous MPs investing and owning Caribbean plantations.

The industrial revolution was almost certainly kick-started by profits generated by the trade of millions of enslaved people, from Africa to the Caribbean. English-owned ships carried at least three million enslaved people to the Caribbean.

When plantation owners decided to retire and returned to England they often brought their servants and domestic enslaved staff back with them. And, as frequently happened, these people could still be sold on, even in London. It became quite fashionable for wealthy households to own black servants, footmen and cooks. Some fortunate enslaved people were able to buy their freedom but often found life hard, as employment was difficult to come by and so they were reduced to begging or crime. Life could be even tougher for freed black women in London.

By 1760, there were at least 10,000 black people living in England and Wales. They were mainly concentrated

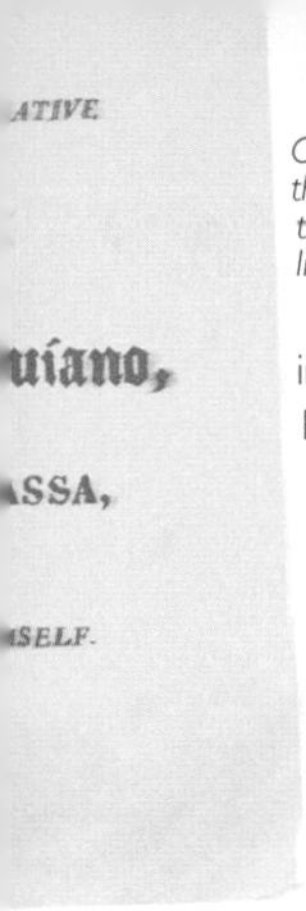

*Clockwise from far left: a plan view of a slave ship revealing the horrific conditions in which enslaved people were held; the title page of Olaudah Equiano's book, a chronicle of his life as an enslaved person; the nurse, Mary Seacole.*

in the larger cities where they had first arrived: Bristol, Liverpool and London. But unlike other recently arrived immigrants, such as Huguenots and Jews, black people did not gather or live in a particular district, they were scattered across the city, often residing in accommodation provided by their enslavers.

**Towards abolition** During the second half of the eighteenth century several campaigns began the process to abolish slavery and free those still enslaved. In England, slavery had never been authorised by law though this was generally ignored when the enslavers arrived back in England, bringing their human chattels with them.

In 1771, James Somerset, who was enslaved in England, escaped but was later captured by his subjugator and imprisoned on a ship destined for Jamaica. His enslaver planned to sell him once in the Caribbean. However, on hearing the news, Somerset's godparents applied to courts for writ of unlawful detention. The court case was brought before Lord Mansfield in early 1772. The abolitionist Granville Sharp and several other lawyers represented Somerset in court. Mansfield eventually ruled that enslaved people could not be legally shipped out of England against their will although they still remain enslaved. Somerset was freed, though the ruling was later ignored or contested.

Inspired by the anti-slavery crusades of former enslaved people turned campaigners, such as Olaudah Equiano and Ottobah Cugoano, the MP William Wilberforce began a 20-year parliamentary campaign to have slavery abolished. It was to be an uphill struggle. When an abolition bill was defeated in Parliament in 1791, church bells rang out in Bristol. The city had literally been built on the proceeds of slavery.

In 1807, Parliament finally passed an act that suppressed the trading of enslaved people, although slavery would not be finally eradicated until the 1833 Slavery Abolition Act was given royal assent. After the act was passed a generation of mainly male, freed slaves almost vanished from London; they were swallowed up by a rapidly expanding city. Some married British women and started families.

**Great Victorians** The first mixed race MP to take a seat in the House of Commons was John Stewart in 1832. It would, however, be another 150 years before a black woman, Diane Abbott, entered the chamber as an MP. She was joined, on the same day in 1997, by three black male MPs.

In 1854, a black woman arrived in London from Jamaica. One hundred and fifty years later she would be voted the 'Greatest Black Briton'. Her name was Mary Seacole, a nurse, who despite the odds took her skills to the battlefields of the Crimean War.

The young, gifted musician Samuel Coleridge-Taylor was born in London in 1875 of mixed race parentage. He would go on to gain a place at the Royal College of Music at the age of 15 and compose *Hiawatha's Wedding Feast* seven years later.

**SS *Empire Windrush*** At the end of the Second World War, Britain needed to rebuild its essential infrastructure including industry, agriculture and housing. Medical care and the railways were about to be nationalised and more staff recruited. Many prisoners of war were offered work and remained to restore the country after the ravages of war.

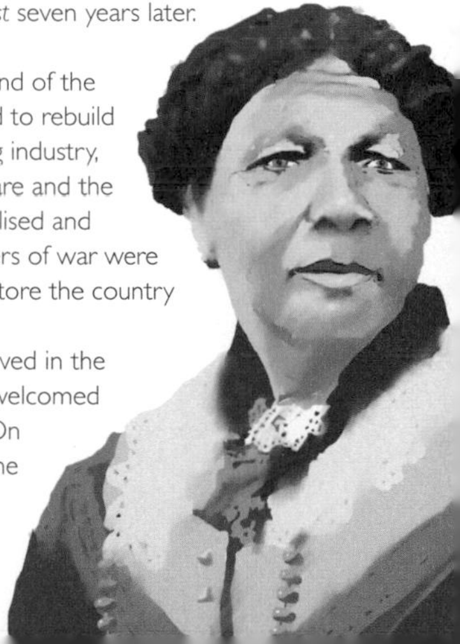

Caribbean soldiers who had served in the Second World War generally felt welcomed by the British during the conflict. On returning to the Caribbean after the war, they discovered 40 per cent unemployment and were shocked by the conditions there, with many vowing to return to Britain. The 1948 Nationalities Act gave those from the colonies and Empire free entry into the UK, and it confirmed their status as British citizens.

In May 1948, a captured Nazi troopship, the SS *Empire Windrush* arrived in Kingston, Jamaica. It was en route from Australia and due to collect servicemen who were on leave. Seeing that the ship wasn't full, the captain of the *Windrush* advertised passages to Britain at a cost of £28.10s (about six months wages for Jamaicans). This was not for the poor but those who could afford it outright or with the assistance of money raised by the family. Among those paying for the passage were former RAF staff, law students and medics. A total of 492 tickets were sold with a few other passengers stowing away.

The British government claimed it had no idea the ship was coming and wasn't prepared, despite 100,000 Poles having recently found employment in the UK. Over the years the *Windrush* became a symbol of a generation of Commonwealth citizens who came to Britain.

In three years, post-war elation had switched to despondency as rationing was in full swing and life had not returned to pre-war standards. The *Windrush* passengers were seeking a better life and work was relatively easy to find. In 1956, London Transport began to actively recruit staff from the Caribbean for their expanding transportation network. Matters were not so good elsewhere; in Bristol, the local bus company simply refused to employ black drivers and conductors. The situation wasn't resolved until the 1965 Race Relations Act was passed.

Sourcing decent accommodation was often a problem for black immigrants. Many landlords simply refused to rent rooms to people of colour. Other landlords, such as Peter Rackman, who was operating in Notting Hill and Paddington, exploited the situation and would rent out single occupancy rooms to several people. These houses and flats often had poor sanitation and meagre heating, for which the tenants were charged exorbitant rent.

Arrivals took comfort in the thought that they would be only in Britain for a few years and then they'd return home. But in most cases, they never did. Their families started to join them and settled. They began to establish roots, regardless of the cold winters and cold attitudes of some locals.

**Notting Hill** By 1958, tensions were running high in Notting Hill as Teddy Boys and supporters of Oswald Mosley's Union Movement launched attacks on black men. It resulted in a race riot in Notting Hill in late August that year. There was no cap on the numbers entering Britain from the Commonwealth and some, like Mosley and his supporters, began to agitate for restrictions to be imposed, and even enforced repatriation.

Politicians eventually responded and drew up the Commonwealth Immigration Act in 1962, which was introduced to slow down immigration.

Seven years after the Notting Hill riots and as a response to the unrest and animosity between some groups of black and white people, the Notting Hill Carnival was born. This two-day festival of music and dance rooted in Caribbean culture has grown into the largest street event in Europe.

**Simmering tensions** By the 1970s, many second-generation black children were expecting more from life than their parents had had to tolerate. Having been brought up and educated in the UK, they wanted better jobs and better houses than those of their parents. But black people, having often taken poorly paid jobs, were frequently the first to be made unemployed when an economic recession hit the country.

Any attempt to organise was seen by certain politicians and the police as a threat. A small restaurant, the Mangrove in Notting Hill became a meeting place for black radicals and celebrities. For the police and Special Branch, this was grounds to repeatedly raid the establishment in search of drugs (none were ever found). Still, the 'Mangrove Nine' were arrested and put on trial. However, the case against them was later dismissed in court.

Between 1976 and 1981, 31 people of colour were murdered in racist attacks in the UK. This included Altab Ali, a Bangladeshi textile worker who was attacked as he walked home in Whitechapel in 1978. Thousands more were attacked and injured during this period, with the police often not taking the reported crimes seriously.

In January 1981, 13 young black people were killed in a house fire, in Deptford. A large demonstration later marched to Whitehall claiming the fire was racially motivated. The police thought it was accidental. The question was never really answered, and tensions between the black community and the police continued to simmer.

**The Brixton Riots and beyond** A few months later matters came to a head after the Metropolitan Police began an operation to question and arrest black people in Brixton. Battles between the Brixton community and police ensued for several days and riots spread across the country. Some years later, riots against the police erupted again in Brixton and Tottenham.

Following the Scarman Report into the 1981 Brixton Riot, the police were still randomly stopping and searching a higher proportion of black people than any minority ethnic group in the UK, even though the 'sus law' had been repealed that year. This report didn't brand the Metropolitan Police as 'institutionally racist'; it would take another public inquiry into the racist murder of 18-year-old Stephen Lawrence, in south-east London in 1993, before this term would appear.

In the USA, following the murders of Trayvon Martin in 2012 and George Floyd in 2021 by policemen, the Black Lives Matter campaign was launched and focused global attention on police violence and racially motivated attacks upon black people. In the UK, the BLM campaign has highlighted the cases of numerous black people, including Mark Duggan, Sean Rigg and Rashan Charles, who have died following incidents with the police.

The many thousands who arrived from the Caribbean in the 1950s, known as the Windrush Generation, have had to battle with the British Home Office over the legality of their rights to live in the UK. Some were illegally deported and many lost their homes and jobs as a result. A legal battle for compensation is still underway.

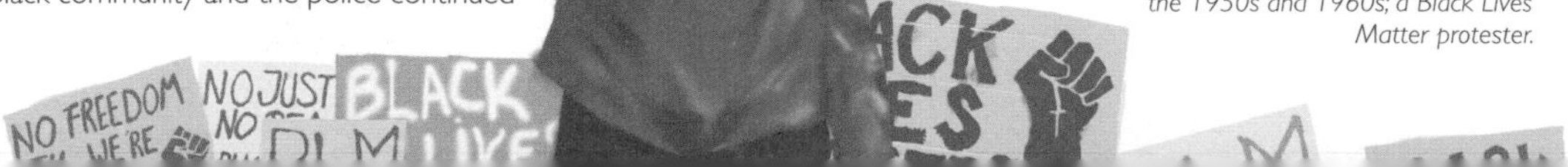

*Clockwise from far left: the SS* Empire Windrush *docks at Tilbury in May 1948;. a typical window sign seen in certain bed and breakfast establishments during the 1950s and 1960s; a Black Lives Matter protester.*

# WEST END

*Total walking distance 8.3km*

This walk through the heart of the West End of the capital features numerous black international musicians, performers, anti-slavery campaigners, the first black QC and a nursing heroine of the Crimean War.

**1 Jimi Hendrix** While the hugely significant blues and experimental rock guitarist and singer Jimi Hendrix was not born a Londoner, he was based in the capital for the final, most influential years of his life. Hendrix was born in Seattle, Washington, in 1942, and went on to record with the likes of Little Richard and the Isley Brothers in his home country before being persuaded by his manager, Chas Chandler, to move to London in 1966. By October that year, he had formed a band, The Jimi Hendrix Experience, with Noel Redding and Mitch Mitchell. Soon afterwards they recorded such trademark tracks as 'Hey Joe' and 'Purple Haze'. The 1967 album *Are You Experienced* was only kept from the number one spot by The Beatles' *Sgt Pepper's Lonely Hearts Club Band*. The Jimi Hendrix Experience would go on to record two further highly acclaimed albums.

Hendrix moved into the top two floors of 23 Brook Street in 1968, with his girlfriend Kathy Etchingham (the house is still standing). The following year, The Jimi Hendrix Experience toured extensively in Europe, the States and headlined at the Woodstock Festival in August.

His last public appearance was at Ronnie Scott's in Frith Street. Sadly, on 18 September 1970, Hendrix died of a drug overdose at the Samarkand Hotel in Notting Hill. He was 27.

**2 Florence Mills Social Parlour** The political activist Amy Ashwood Garvey was born in Jamaica in 1897. Together with her husband Marcus Garvey, she founded the United Negro Improvement Association with the aim of working for the development of people of African origin around the globe *(page 74)*.

Ashwood Garvey was later the treasurer of the International African Friends of Abyssinians (IAFA). In 1935, after Mussolini's Fascist army had invaded Abyssinia (Ethiopia), it was she and the IAFA that greeted the deposed leader, Haile Selassie, when he arrived in London. Ashwood Garvey was also an advocate of black women working within the political arena. Along with Sam Manning, a calypso singer, Ashwood Garvey established The Florence Mills Social Parlour at 50 Carnaby Street in 1936, as a social forum and restaurant for black writers, intellectuals, artists and musicians. The club was named after the black American cabaret singer and dancer, Florence Mills, who was also an outspoken advocate of equal rights for African Americans.

**3 Mary Seacole** Mary Seacole was a nurse whose healing efforts in the field hospitals of the Crimean War (1853–1856) rivalled those of Florence Nightingale. Seacole was briefly recognised for her labours immediately after the war but her name soon faded, outshone by the deeds of 'the lady with the lamp'. It is only recently that her deeds and efforts have been recognised once more.



Seacole was born in Jamaica in 1805, to a Scottish father and a Jamaican mother who ran a boarding house for convalescing military officers and was a practitioner of traditional herbal medicine. Mary was soon helping her mother and acquiring many of her healing skills. She travelled widely, enhancing her nursing skills especially for the treatment of cholera and yellow fever. In 1854, she was in London when news broke of injured soldiers in the Crimean War receiving poor care. Seacole approached the War Office with an offer to help but was rebutted, possibly on the grounds of her ethnicity, even though vacancies existed within Nightingale's operation.

Undeterred, she made her own way to the Crimea with a business partner, to establish a hotel and store near the British camp. The hotel, built from scavenged pieces of timber and iron, became quite a success among the infantry, as 'Mother Seacole's' reputation spread, not only for the food and beverages she served in the midst of battle but also her care of the injured. Even some of the military doctors acknowledged her caring and nursing skills, especially her treatment of cholera victims.

At the end of the war Seacole's hotel was redundant, and as she could not readily move the stock back to London, the business was declared bankrupt. *The Times* newspaper commented in late 1856 *'While the benevolent deeds of Florence Nightingale are being handed down to posterity … are the humbler actions of Mrs Seacole to be entirely forgotten?'*

Pricked by guilt, two British army commanders arranged a four-day musical festival in 1857 in honour and support of Seacole. However, after expenses it only raised £57. Seacole died in 1881 and was buried in the Roman Catholic section of the Kensal Green Cemetery. In 2004, she was voted the greatest black Briton. Numerous buildings and hospital wards are now named after her in tribute to her selfless work on the battlefield.

*Clockwise from far left: Jimi Hendrix; a plaque at 14 Soho Square where Mary Seacole lived from 1857 to 1860; Mary Seacole; a Carnaby Street sign.*

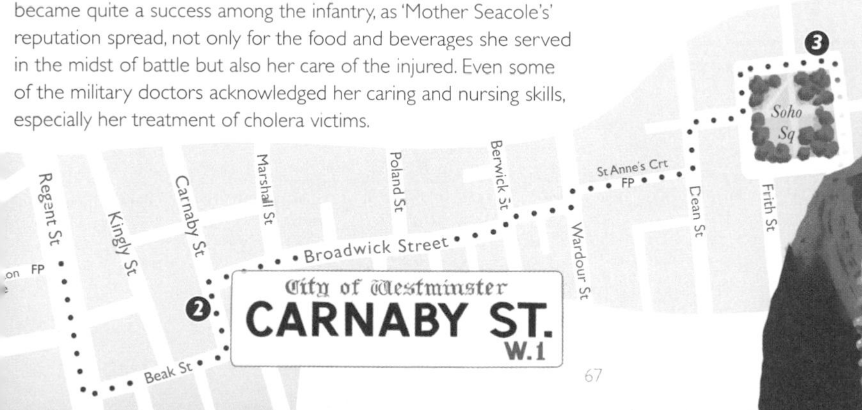

**1 Nadia Cattouse** One of the first black actors to appear in a BBC drama was Nadia Cattouse. She also became a pioneer of radio and folk music. Cattouse was born in Belize in 1924 and during the Second World War she came to Britain to serve as a signals operator. Following the war she undertook teacher training in Glasgow and on returning home she took up the post of headmistress.

In 1951 she returned to Britain to study at the London School of Economics. In her final year of studies, she was 'spotted' for her singing and acting skills and she was invited to join a variety show. Soon afterwards she successfully auditioned at the BBC. Cattouse went on to appear in television dramas including *Dixon of Dock Green* and *Play for Today*. In 1961, she presented the BBC radio programme *Woman's Hour*. One of the subjects for discussion was interracial marriage. Cattouse had recently married David Lindup, a music arranger and composer. She also worked actively as an anti-racism campaigner.

Cattouse later became known as a folk-singer of repute, appearing at the Les Cousins Folk and Blues Club at 49 Greek Street during the late 1960s (the building is now the 49 Club). *Melody Maker* referred to her as 'one of the giants of the folk-song revival in Britain'. Her son, Mike Lindup, also became a musician and was keyboard player in the band Level 42.

**2 Elisabeth Welch** It was at the Leicester Square Theatre (no longer standing) in 1933 that Elisabeth Welch made her London debut, in a production of the revue *Dark Doings* in which she sang the Cole Porter number 'Stormy Weather', a song that would become her signature tune. Welch was born in New Jersey in 1904 and by the age of 18 she had already appeared on the Broadway stage as a singer before heading to Europe to pursue her career. In 1928, while in Paris she performed in cabaret with Florence Mill's Blackbirds at the Moulin Rouge.

Back in New York, Welch appeared in Cole Porter's musical *The New Yorkers* in 1930, which featured the then controversial song 'Love for Sale'. In 1933, she had her own musical series *Soft Lights and Sweet Music* on BBC radio and it made her a household name in Britain. Consequently, in 1936, she appeared in an early live television broadcast from Alexandra Palace. She remained in Britain and continued to perform.

In 1979, Welch appeared in Derek Jarman's film version of Shakespeare's *The Tempest* as a goddess singing appropriately 'Stormy Weather'. By 1986, she had appeared in her second Royal Variety Performance at the London Palladium. Following a career spanning over 65 years, she died in 2003.

**3 Paul Robeson** In 1928, the bass-baritone singer and actor Paul Robeson appeared at the Theatre Royal in Drury Lane performing the character of Joe in the acclaimed musical *Showboat*. Robeson was born in New Jersey in 1898, the son of an enslaved person. He trained as a lawyer but because of his ethnicity he was prohibited from practising law. Though Robeson only lived for around 12 years in London, he is worthy of inclusion since he became a powerful advocate of black civil rights and anti-colonialism, and was a political activist. In 1930, at the Savoy Theatre, Robeson played the lead role in the Shakespeare play *Othello*, for which he received critical acclaim.

Following a visit to Russia in 1934, his left-wing opinions were only reinforced. By the 1950s, during the McCarthy purges, the US authorities took a dim view of his 'Communist' leanings and withdrew his passport thus confining him to the USA. His music and films were also banned. In 1958, his passport was returned to him and he was free to travel again. The following year he sang in St Paul's Cathedral; the first black performer ever to sing there.

**Note:** Access to Lincoln's Inn is limited to office hours, Monday to Friday.

*Clockwise from top left: Elisabeth Welch; 2 Stone Buildings where Dr John Roberts QC established his own chambers; the singer and actor Paul Robeson.*

**4 Dr John Roberts QC** For a man of many legal firsts, Dr John Roberts QC was an extraordinarily humble and modest man. He was born in Sierra Leone in 1928, of parents whose descendants had returned to Africa after liberation from slavery. In 1964, after ten years in the RAF and a brief spell working for air traffic control in his home country, Roberts returned to Britain and began work as a civil servant while also studying law part time. Law was clearly to become his vocation as in 1969 he was called to the bar (as a barrister) and became Master of the Bench in 1972. He would eventually be called to the bar in nine Caribbean countries.

Roberts was the first person of African descent to establish his own Chambers in 1975, at 2 Stone Buildings, where he employed African, Caribbean, Asian and white members of staff. Roberts accepted seven female barristers to work within his Chamber; something quite unheard of at the time. In 1988, he became the first person of African ancestry to be appointed a QC at the English Bar and in 1992 he became a high court judge in the Supreme Courts of the British Virgin Islands. Among the many honours Roberts received are the Freedom of the City of London in 1996 and a CBE in 2011. He died in 2016.

*Walking these pages 2.6km*

**1 Samuel Coleridge-Taylor** A young gifted 'Anglo-African' composer, Samuel Coleridge-Taylor became the first black person to make a major contribution to British concert music.

Coleridge-Taylor was born at 15 Theobalds Road, Holborn, in 1875. His father, Daniel Taylor, was a doctor from Sierra Leone. Before his third birthday Samuel had moved, with his mother Alice Holman, to Croydon. His father did not follow them. There were many musicians in the Holman's extended family and soon Coleridge-Taylor was learning the violin. At the young age of 15 the talented Coleridge-Taylor had commenced his seven-year education at the Royal College of Music (RCM), where he would study composition.

In 1898, Coleridge-Taylor, now aged 22, scored Hiawatha's Wedding Feast, based on Longfellow's epic poem, *The Song of Hiawatha*. The cantata was first performed in the same year and it received critical acclaim. Sir Hubert Parry, principal of the RCM, proclaimed after the concert it was *'one of the most remarkable events in modern English musical history'*. Coleridge-Taylor would receive no royalties for 'Hiawatha's Wedding Feast' as he had signed away his rights for an initial one-off fee.

He travelled to the USA several times in the early twentieth century where he had become a hero figure to many black people. His concerts were sell-outs and he received numerous ovations. He met the African-American poet Paul Laurence Dunbar and put some of his works to music, drawing much from his father's ancestry. He was even invited to meet President Franklin D. Roosevelt at the White House. This was a much better reception compared to some of the abuse he received from racist groups at home. A Church of England canon was reported to have said to Coleridge-Taylor *'it really is surprising: you eat like we do, dress like we do and talk as we do'*. The composer later wrote *'There is an appalling amount of ignorance among the English people regarding the Negro and his doing…'*

Between the wars, 'Hiawatha's Wedding Feast' was performed each year at the Royal Albert Hall, conducted by Malcolm Sargent. Sadly, Coleridge-Taylor never lived to see this as he died of pneumonia in 1912, aged 37.

**2 Sir Trevor McDonald** Probably one of the most iconic and best-known television presenters of the news in Britain, Sir Trevor McDonald was born in Trinidad and Tobago in 1939. He worked in print and broadcast journalism before moving to London in 1969 as a BBC producer.

He joined ITN in 1973 and began working as a sports reporter then a sports journalist and rose through the ranks to become the sole anchor for ITN's *News at Ten* broadcasts until it was dropped from the schedules in 1999. He returned briefly to re-launch *News at Ten* before retiring in 2008 from the show. In his time McDonald has interviewed numerous world leaders, including Nelson Mandela, Bill Clinton and Saddam Hussein. He has written biographies of the cricketers Clive Lloyd and Viv Richards and was knighted in 1999.

*Clockwise from top left: Samuel Coleridge-Taylor; Sir Learie Constantine; Dr Harold Moody; Sir Trevor McDonald*

**3 Sir Learie Constantine** The renowned all-round cricketer, captain of the West Indies team and a statesman, Sir Learie Constantine went on to become Britain's first black peer. He was born in Trinidad in 1901 and from an early age showed great potential as a cricketer. He toured England with the West Indies team and in 1928 he signed for the Lancastrian cricket club, Nelson, where he remained for nine years.

In 1943, when he and his family were on a visit to London, they were only allowed a one-night stay at the Imperial Hotel in Russell Square, despite having booked four nights in advance. The manageress was openly racist to Constantine and said that 'blacks were not welcome' in the establishment. He later sued the hotel and won the case. Though the court verdict was very clear, such racist views were still rife, and people of colour could still be refused a room in a hotel or a restaurant table until the 1965 Race Relations Act was introduced. Constantine would go on to sit on the Race Relations Board.

After his cricket playing days were over, Constantine went on to study law and was able to pay for his tuition by coaching. He was finally called to the bar in 1954, the same year he returned to Trinidad and went into politics. By 1961, he was appointed Trinidad and Tobago's first High Commissioner in London, and a year later the Queen knighted him. In 1969 he became Baron Constantine and thus the first black peer in the UK. He passed away in 1971.



**4 Dr Harold Moody** In Great Russell Street in 1931, Dr Harold Moody, with other members of the Central YMCA, established Britain's first civil rights movement, the League of Coloured Peoples (LCP). Original members included C L R James, Paul Robeson and Jomo Kenyatta.

Moody was born in Jamaica in 1882 and in 1904 he came to England to study medicine at King's College, yet despite his glowing academic results he was denied a post at King's due to his skin colour. Faced with such anti-black racism he instead opened his first medical practice in Peckham.

Moody was a great orator and Christian and he grew tired of the stream of anti-black racism, both direct and subtle, that he and fellow black people experienced, especially in the areas of employment and housing. It led him to found the LCP in 1931 and become its president. The LCP was a pressure group that would lobby MPs and write letters to the media.

In one instance Moody wrote to the BBC following the use of the word 'n**ger' by a radio announcer. Given his status, the response by the Corporation was swift and very apologetic. However, this approach did not appeal to all black people, some of whom preferred a more radical approach to racism in the 1930s.

During the Second World War Harold Moody continued his work as a GP in the Peckham area, assisting with victims of bombing attacks. Following a long lecture tour of North America in 1947 he contracted influenza and died. His younger brother was the artist Ronald Moody.

***1* Mary Prince** Born into slavery in 1788 on the island of Bermuda, Mary Prince went on to become a major figure in the campaign to abolish slavery. During her childhood she was sold several times, worked in horrendous conditions and often suffered abuse at the hands of her enslavers. In 1815, she was sold on again to John Adams Wood of Antigua, where she worked as an enslaved domestic. Prince joined the Moravian Church where she learned to read and write and married her husband, a freed slaved person; an act for which her enslaver beat her.

The Wood family returned to London in 1828 and took Prince with them as a servant. Following the Somerset versus Stewart case of 1772 *(page 63)*, enslaved people once in England could no longer be removed from the country. Eventually Woods granted Prince the formal right to leave but did not grant her freedom. She fled the household to the Moravian church in Hatton Garden and there met Thomas Pringle, an active member of the Anti-Slavery Society. If Prince had wanted to be with her husband in Antigua then she would have to become enslaved again. The Anti-Slavery Society petitioned Parliament on behalf of Prince to be freed from slavery, but the petition was turned down.

In 1829, encouraged by Pringle, Prince began working as a servant in his house in Malet Street while also transcribing her experiences as an enslaved person (the site, marked with a plaque, is now occupied by the University Senate Building). The book was published in 1831 and entitled *The History of Mary Prince*. It was the first printed account of a black woman's life in slavery, and it became one of several key influences in the campaign for the abolition of slavery. In 1833, the Slavery Abolition Act was passed and became law, abolishing the act of slavery across most of the British Empire. Even though the enslavers were compensated financially for their loss of free labour, the act had a huge effect on the economics of the Caribbean. The enslaved themselves were not recompensed. Little is known about Mary Prince after 1833.

THE

HISTORY OF MARY PRINCE,

A WEST INDIAN SLAVE.

RELATED BY HERSELF.

WITH A SUPPLEMENT BY THE EDITOR.

To which is added,

THE NARRATIVE OF ASA-ASA,

A CAPTURED AFRICAN.

***2* Bob Marley** In 1972, the singer Johnny Nash invited the then largely unknown Bob Marley and the Wailers to tour with him in Britain. While in London at this time, Marley lived at 34 Ridgmont Gardens (a plaque now marks the flat). Three years later, with a re-formed band, Marley recorded and released their first internationally successful song 'No Woman, No Cry' on the influential Island Records label. Following an attempt on Marley's life in Jamaica, he moved to London – by now the capital was his second home.

In 1977, while living at 42 Oakley Street, Chelsea, Marley completed the album *Exodus*, which was released to critical acclaim. In the same year he was diagnosed with a skin melanoma, yet despite the illness he and the band continued to record and tour. In late 1980, with declining health, Marley eventually sought treatment at a German clinic but it was too late; he died of cancer the following year, at the age of 36.

**3 Olaudah Equiano** The erudite Olaudah Equiano became an early advocate for the abolition of slavery. As a former enslaved person, he was able, through his writing and campaigning, to bring attention to the horrors of slavery to a largely unaware British public.

Equiano was born in Nigeria around 1745 and by the age of 11 he has been kidnapped by enslavers and shipped to the Caribbean. In Virginia, he was sold to a British naval officer, Michael Pascal, who transported him to England in 1757. He accompanied him during many battles in the Seven Year War. Later, under the supervision of Pascal's sisters, he was taught to read and write. Equiano was baptised in St Margaret's Church, Westminster, in 1759. Finally, in 1767, for the fee of £40 he was able to buy his freedom, and then spent the next few years crewing on various sailing expeditions across the globe and was even captured and temporarily placed back into slavery. On his return to London, Equiano became increasingly involved with the abolition of slavery movement in England. He was an excellent campaigner and public speaker, and he met with Granville Sharp, the chairman of the Quaker Society's radical campaign to abolish slavery. Equiano toured the country speaking on behalf of the abolitionists.

In 1789, Equiano, encouraged by Sharp, wrote his autobiography *The Interesting Narrative of the Life of Olaudah Equiano, or Gustava Vassa* the African* while living at 37 Tottenham Street (**3a**) and later at Riding House Street (**3b**). It was a chronicle of his life as an enslaved person. The book, a bestseller, reached a large audience and activated public attitude against slavery. It was reprinted numerous times, with the author becoming a leader and spokesman for the black enslaved people within the British Empire. In 1781, he alerted Sharp and the press to the massacre of the 132 enslaved, who were thrown overboard the Liverpool slave ship *Zong*. The owners of the ship had tried to claim insurance money for the loss. He also wrote damning reviews of pamphlets published by anti-abolitionists, who were attempting to maintain the status quo of slavery in the Caribbean.

Equiano died in 1797 aged around 52. The first parliamentary act to abolish the slave trade was still ten years away but he had furnished William Wilberforce MP with the moral ammunition to see the act through. Equiano's body was buried in the churchyard of the Whitfield Tabernacle on Tottenham Court Road. It is now the site of the American International Church (**3c**).

**Gustave Vassa was a name given to him by one of his enslavers.*

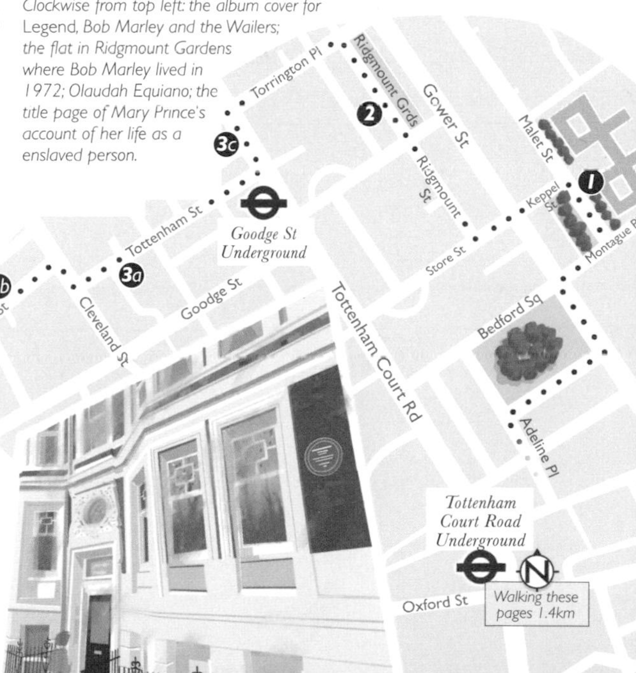


*Clockwise from top left: the album cover for Legend, Bob Marley and the Wailers; the flat in Ridgmount Gardens where Bob Marley lived in 1972; Olaudah Equiano; the title page of Mary Prince's account of her life as a enslaved person.*

# NOTTING HILL

*Total walking distance 3.1km*

Attracted by cheap accommodation, a community of largely Trinidadian migrants established itself in post-war Notting Hill and North Kensington. For the newcomer, life was not always comfortable.

**1 The Notting Hill riots** By the end of the Second World War, men and women from all parts of the Commonwealth were being encouraged to travel to the UK to assist with the reconstruction of the country's infrastructure. Ten years later, certain British-born white groups were unhappy with the rate of immigration, especially from the West Indies, claiming that immigrants were 'stealing' their jobs (and even 'their' women), at a time when unemployment was beginning to rise. The fascist Union Movement led by Oswald Mosley campaigned to 'Keep Britain White'.

Sporadic violence against Afro-Caribbean men, when often out late at night and alone, especially in areas such as Notting Hill became commonplace. 'Teddy Boys' (or Teds – young white working-class men dressed in mock Edwardian clothing with quiffed hairstyles) saw themselves as 'guardians' of the white race.

A race riot had occurred in Nottingham on 23 August 1958. Teds were out looking to attack black men and if they didn't find anyone they often, bizarrely, attacked each other instead.

The situation in Notting Dale (a residential area in Notting Hill) the following Saturday was febrile, with Teds coming into the area looking for trouble. It then exploded that night as over 300 white youths attacked a house just off Bramley Road where a party of mainly Afro-Caribbean people was taking place. Sporadic incidents flared up across Notting Hill. The Teddy Boys attacked with petrol bombs, bottles and knives. The riots were now on national television news, which only attracted more troublemakers. The police were unprepared and unable to quell the mayhem. As the West Indian people tried to protect themselves, they fought back, and the riots continued for several nights.

Nine white youths were arrested and charged. They each received heavy sentences of four years' imprisonment. The West Indian community gained respect from the general population: they were not pushovers and they were here to stay. However, calls were made by some politicians to end the high level of immigration.

**2 Amy Ashwood Garvey** The pan-African activist and feminist Amy Ashwood became the first wife of Marcus Garvey when they married in New York in 1919. Though the marriage only lasted three years, Amy never accepted the divorce and kept the Garvey surname. She moved to London in 1934 and two years later took residence at 1 Bassett Road, living here until 1960 *(page 66)*

**3 Kelso Cochrane's murder** Antiguan-born Kelso Cochrane, a 32-year-old carpenter, was returning from hospital on 17 May 1959, having received treatment for a work-related injury, when a gang of young, white Teddy Boys set upon him outside 36 Golborne Road. He was racially insulted, punched and stabbed, and later died in hospital. A memorial plaque now marks the spot of his murder. The police, believing the motive for the attack was robbery, arrested two 19-year-olds, but later released them. The police enquiries met a wall of silence from within the North Kensington community, and the coroner concluded that Cochrane's murder had not been racially motivated. Cochrane's funeral attracted over 1,000 mourners, who followed the coffin to Kensal Green Cemetery. His killers were never found. Cochrane's murder galvanised the growing campaign against attacks by racist gangs in the UK and the demand for anti-discrimination laws to be introduced.

**4 Island Studios** This Romanesque building was a former church facing Lancaster Road. It later became home to Island Records Studio. In 1977, Bob Marley and the Wailers *(page 72)* recorded the acclaimed album *Exodus* here.

**5 The Mangrove Nine** In December 1971, a group of black activists known as the Mangrove Nine were acquitted of the charge of riotous assembly. It was alleged that they had attacked 24 policemen during a demonstration in West Kilburn a year earlier. They were protesting against the police harassment of restaurant owner Frank Crichlow (one of the Nine). Crichlow was a successful Trinidadian businessman who had arrived in London in the 1950s. His establishment, The Mangrove, was located at 8 All Saints Road and it became a meeting point for black rights activists and celebrities alike. The police raided The Mangrove 12 times between 1969 and 1970, looking for drugs or weapons, but none were ever found. The raids were seen by many as yet more police harassment.

Several of those charged, including the broadcaster and campaigner, Darcus Howe, defended themselves at the Old Bailey. The others were represented by the anti-racism barrister Ian Macdonald QC. The trial succeeded in highlighting racism within the Metropolitan Police.

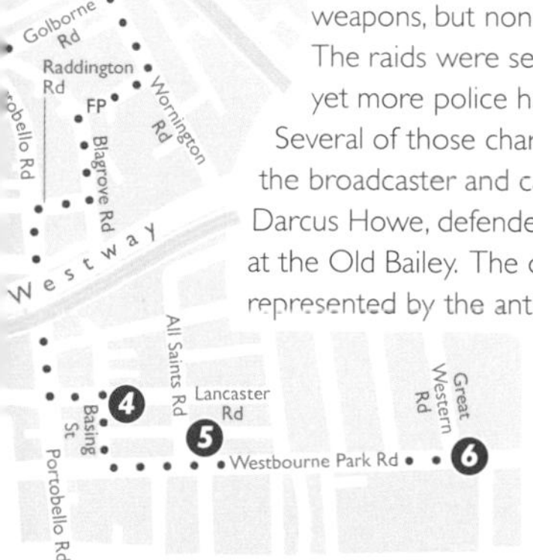


*Clockwise from left: 'Battle For Freedom' – a campaign poster for the Mangrove Nine; drummers at the Notting Hill Carnival; the former Island Records Studio in Basing Street.*

**6 The Notting Hill Carnival** As a response to the 1958 Notting Hill race riots, Claudia Jones established the *West Indian Gazette*, the first large circulation black newspaper in the UK. In February 1959, she also organised a Caribbean carnival of music and dance in St Pancras Town Hall.

Seven years later, Rhaune Laslett coordinated a Caribbean street event in Notting Hill, with steel bands and dancers; its aim was to celebrate London's multicultural diversity. The Carnivals of the 1970s saw the event expanding with more steel bands, reggae groups and louder sound systems. The number of people attending also began to increase dramatically.

The 1976 Notting Hill Carnival was marred when heavy-handed policing irritated some Afro-Caribbean youths, who responded with bottle throwing. In the year 2000, two men were murdered during the festival and consequently the Carnival began to receive considerable negative press coverage. However, it has survived and is now the largest street event in Europe, with over two million people attending the two-day event. Despite attempts to move the event into Hyde Park, the unique August Bank holiday Carnival still circles the streets of Notting Hill each year. Westbourne Park Road is on the Carnival route .

*Walking these pages 3.1km*

# WESTMINSTER

*Total walking distance 2.2km*

This walk through the home of British government and power reveals several influential people who campaigned for the abolition of slavery plus black parliamentarians and an American civil rights campaigner.

**1 Ottobah Cugoano** Around 1760, at the age of 13, Cugoano was kidnapped in Ghana and shipped to Grenada in the Caribbean and put to work as a plantation enslaved person. In 1772, two years after being brought to London, Cugoano was given his freedom. He changed his name to John Stuart and became an assistant to the painter Richard Cosway, whose studio was within the fine residence of Schlomberg House, at 82 Pall Mall. It was here, in 1787, that Cugoano wrote and published his '*Thoughts and sentiments on the evil and wicked traffic of the slavery and commerce of the human species*'. In the book he demolished the arguments of the time that slavery had divine sanction and Africans were 'suited' to slavery. Cugoano asserted that enslaved people had a moral right to resist. This was the first book written by a former enslaved person on the subject of abolition. It is believed that he wrote it with the assistance of Olaudah Equiano *(page 73)* – a fellow of the abolitionist group, the Sons of Africa. Two years later Equiano would write his own volume on the evils of slavery. Little is known about Cugoano after 1791. It is possible that he died soon after. A plaque marks the house on Pall Mall.

**2 Charles Ignatius Sancho** Life for Sancho started badly; within a year of his birth (on a slave ship) both his parents were dead. In 1731, at the age of two, he was despatched from Ecuador to his new owner's sisters in Greenwich.

The Duke of Montagu, a friend of the sisters, met and encouraged the young Sancho to educate himself. The sisters were not so keen for his improvement and, in frustration, Sancho ran away to join the Montagu household in 1749. When he wasn't working as a valet, Sancho began writing plays and musical compositions, several of which were published. He became friends with the author of *Tristram Shandy*, Lawrence Sterne, who encouraged him to lobby for the abolition of slavery.

Following the death of both the duke and duchess, Sancho was left a sum of £30 a year, which he squandered on gambling and the theatre. Almost penniless and afflicted by gout, in 1774, he set up a grocers shop in what is now King Charles Street (a plaque marks the spot). It was from here that Sancho established an ex-enslaved society, and probably where he met Cugoano. Being a man of property he was able to vote and became the first black man to do so. Sancho was a prolific letter writer and an anthology collection was published after his death in 1780. He was buried in the nearby St Margaret's Church.

**3 Statue of Martin Luther King, Jr.** Following the restoration of the western towers of Westminster Abbey in 1995, a decision was taken to fill the ten empty niches above the portal with religious martyrs of the twentieth century. Included in this gathering was a statue of the American civil rights campaigner and minister Martin Luther King, Jr.

*Clockwise from far left: a detail of an engraving by Richard Cosworth featuring his assistant Ottobah Cugoano serving grapes; Diane Abbott, the first black female MP; the Houses of Parliament; the Buxton Memorial; the tombstone of William Wilberforce inside Westminster Abbey; a memorial to Martin Luther King, Jr. on the west portal of Westminster Abbey; Ignatius Sancho.*

**4 The tomb of William Wilberforce** By the time the body of anti-slavery campaigner William Wilberforce was laid to rest in Westminster Abbey* in July 1833, his humanitarian crusade was nearly complete. Within a few months the Slavery Abolition Act had gained royal assent.

In the late 1780s, as an MP, Wilberforce had been introduced to several leading anti-slavery campaigners, including Thomas Clarkson. He collected evidence from numerous quarters, including the Society for the Abolition of the Slave Trade and from Ottobah Cugoano and Olaudah Equiano *(page 73)*, both former enslaved persons who had written about their experiences.

The first attempt to get the Abolition of the Slave Trade Act through Parliament in 1791 failed. The following year, 500 petitions were delivered to Parliament in support of Wilberforce's campaign. Finally, in 1807, the act ultimately was passed after 20 years of procedure.

** An entrance fee is charged.*

**5 Black parliamentarians** In 1832, John Stewart entered the Commons as the first mixed race MP. He inherited a sugar plantation in British Guiana from his father that, until 1833, forced over 400 people into a life of slavery. It would take another 155 years before the first black woman would enter Parliament as an MP. Diane Abbott was elected as MP for Hackney North and Stoke Newington in the Labour landslide of 1987. Abbott was born in London to Jamaican parents. On the same day that she was elected she was joined by three other MPs of colour: Bernie Grant, Keith Vaz and Paul Boateng, who also became the first black cabinet minister. In the House of Lords, Sir Learie Constantine became the first black peer in 1969 *(page 71)*. Baroness Amos became the first black life peer in 1997 and the first black woman to serve as a cabinet minister.

**6 Buxton Memorial** This odd neo-gothic former drinking fountain was commissioned by Charles Buxton MP as a memorial to commemorate the efforts of his father, Sir Thomas Fowler Buxton, along with Wilberforce and Clarkson, in securing the abolition of slavery. Bizarrely, the memorial used to feature former royal rulers of England until they 'disappeared'. No reference is made of the 12 million people who were forcibly enslaved.

*Walking these pages 2.2km*

WILLIAM WILBERFORCE
BORN 24TH AUGUST 1759
DIED 29TH JULY 1833

# BRIXTON

*Total walking distance 4.5km*

In 1948, a relatively small number of Jamaicans arrived in Brixton and settled, and from this nucleus many more followed, creating a large Caribbean community. A generation later, relations between this group and the police were far from good.

***1* The 1981 Brixton Riots** In early 1981, 13 young black people were killed in a house fire in Deptford. The cause of the fire was never determined. Several months later, the Metropolitan Police began Operation Swamp 81 in Brixton because of increased robberies in the area. Plain clothes police and the Special Patrol Group began to stop and search mainly black people without good reason. They were applying the 'sus law', under which a police officer could arrest somebody, without evidence, on suspicion that they had committed a crime. The much despised law was used throughout the 1970s to harass black and other ethnic minority groups in the UK.

On 10 April 1981, the police stopped a shirtless black man on Railton Road who had just been stabbed. About 50 black people gathered at the site of the incident, followed quickly by more police, now in riot gear. The injured man was taken to hospital.

The following day, Saturday, some activists arrived from other parts of the country, along with the media, sensing that something was about to erupt. During the afternoon a black minicab driver was stopped, also on Railton Road, on suspicion of carrying drugs. His car was searched. Meanwhile, a crowd of black people gathered and began to throw bricks at police and their vehicles. One police car was burnt-out. Skirmishes between black (and some white) youths and the police then erupted simultaneously all over Brixton, which resulted in nearly 360 police and members of the public being injured. Many cars and buildings were damaged and shops looted. The rioting did not end until Monday evening.

Later, during the summer of 1981, riots erupted in many towns and cities, with battles being fought between the police and mainly youths. Unlike the Notting Hill Riots of 1958 *(page 74)* this was not a black versus white matter; this was alienated youths, both black and white, against the police.

The government commissioned Lord Scarman to produce a report into the cause of the unrest. In his summary he found that black people in Brixton and elsewhere were living in deprivation, social despair and suffering at the hands of racist groups. At the time, half of black youths between the ages of 16 and 19 in Brixton were unemployed.

**2 The 1985 Brixton Riots** During a police raid on 28 September 1985, to arrest Michael Groce in connection with an earlier robbery, the officers accidentally shot his mother, Cherry Groce, at her house in north Brixton. As news of this shooting spread, skirmishes between the police and local youths erupted. Several cars were set alight on Brixton Road, Branksome Road (**2b**) and Acre Lane. Despite the implementation of the Scarman Report, tensions between the local black population and the police were still febrile.

Rioters threw petrol bombs at Brixton police station (**2a**). One building and numerous cars were destroyed in the disturbances and the police arrested 230 people for violence, burglary and theft following two days of rioting.



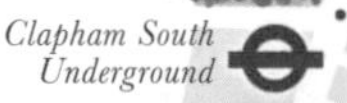

Many of those detained were white. A photojournalist died a few days after being attacked by rioters. Mrs Groce was paralysed as a result of the shooting and lived until 2011.

**3 Electric Avenue** This street got its name as it was one of the first streets in the UK to be illuminated by electricity. Glass canopies once covered the footpath. Today it is now a popular street food market, selling produce from the Caribbean, Asia, Africa and South America. Motivated by the 1981 Brixton Riots, Eddy Grant wrote the hit song 'Electric Avenue'.

**4 The Sharpeville Memorial** In Windrush Square stands a memorial stone to the 69 people killed in the Sharpeville Massacre. In 1960, during an anti-apartheid demonstration in Sharpeville, South Africa, the police panicked and began shooting into the unarmed crowd. The massacre alerted the world to the horrors of the apartheid regime.

**5 Black Cultural Archives** The Black Cultural Archives (BCA) was established in 1981, to portray and celebrate the history and culture of black British people. This heritage centre in Brixton was established by the activist, historian and educationalist Len Garrison and opened in 2014. The BCA comprises a gallery and a library of material relating to the history of black people through a variety of old and new media.

**6 The Clapham South Underground Shelter** In June 1948, the *Empire Windrush* arrived from the West Indies carrying 492 Jamaicans in search of work and a better life. Around half the arrivals already had employment but for those who didn't, accommodation was offered in a former underground war shelter on Clapham Common, at the rate of 2/6d per night (12.5p). This was temporary accommodation until they had sourced work. The nearest labour exchange was on Coldharbour Lane in nearby Brixton. Through this facility many found work in the Brixton area. The majority of those who had arrived on the *Windrush* were skilled workers, some of whom had served in the forces during the war. They were prepared to take less skilled employment to escape conditions in Jamaica.

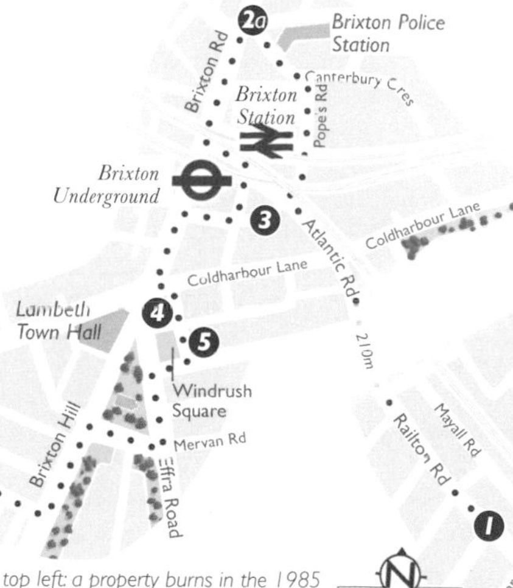

*Clockwise from top left: a property burns in the 1985 Brixton Riots; Electric Avenue street market; the Clapham South Underground shelter entrance.*

# IRISH LONDON

Life for many early Irish immigrants arriving in London (and the rest of England) in the twelfth century was tough. Following an edict issued by Henry III, if they were caught begging they would be expelled from the country. Yet many Irish people were only here because Henry's grandfather, Henry II, had invaded Ireland in 1169 and had made their lives so miserable, through confiscation of their lands, that thousands emigrated to England in search of work. The English political and military hold on Ireland would last for another 750 years and reduce the Irish to second-class citizens in their own country. Over the years there was a steady stream of workers, writers and gentry into England, who were either fleeing wars or seeking employment.

In 1801, the Irish Parliament was dissolved and the country governed from London. Ireland became part of the Union and the Irish became British citizens.

**The Irish Famine** The industrial revolution that was sweeping across Britain in the 1840s only really took hold in sections of Dublin and Belfast. The vast majority of the Irish population continued to work on the land. Many smallholdings were producing just enough food, usually potatoes, for themselves and their family.

Ireland had suffered potato crop failures in the past but nothing on the scale that would strike in 1847. Two years earlier, a ship carrying a cargo of blighted potatoes docked in Ireland. The effects of the contagion that followed were dramatic. The potato harvest was greatly reduced in 1846, especially in the south and west of the country.

The London government did initially offer some relief to the starving but, following the election of a new Whig government, they placed responsibility for the problems on the absent landlords, and sent in the army to quell the growing unrest. With a lack of food and no other means of income many smallholders were evicted and made homeless. Those who could headed to the workhouse, while many died of starvation or disease. Whole villages were abandoned and in some districts, former potato fields became makeshift graveyards.

By 1847, matters got no better when the potato crop failed again. A lack of Irish Home Rule exacerbated the situation, while the London government still refused to assist yet ensured that other Irish produce, such as meat and vegetables, were still shipped to Britain. By now many local inhabitants were too ill or weak to protest. Those who could packed up what little they had and began the long trek to either Britain, the USA or Australia.

**The Aftermath** Between 1847 and 1851 over a million Irish people died as a result of the famine, and around 1.75 million left Ireland. Being closer, it was cheaper to emigrate to Britain, although many Irish people used Britain as a stepping stone to the USA. A member of the family would head to America, obtain work and send back money to pay for the rest of the family to follow. However, this caused resentment among the 'welcoming' British hosts.

For those who chose to stay in London life was extremely hard. Many Irish people could not speak English, and the transition from a rural way of life to survival in an urban world was tough. They took what menial jobs they could find and lived within the dilapidated rookeries of St Giles, Marylebone, Wapping, Seven Dials and Whitechapel. They chose these areas as rents were cheap and they were often close to sources of employment: the docks and fruit and vegetable markets.

*Left: following the Irish potato famine, many villages were abandoned. Right: the Famine Memorial by Rowan Gillespie, located at Custom House Quay, Dublin.*

Irish immigrants were commonly viewed by some sectors of the British press as being drunk, filthy, ferocious and idle. In 1847, *The Times* described the Irish incomers as *'a fetid mass of famine, nakedness, dirt and fever'*. They did the tough, dirty, back-breaking jobs, such as digging the canals, working the land and hauling coal. Many English working class saw the Irish as a threat to their jobs as they believed they undercut their hourly rates of pay. However, in London, anti-Irish feeling never became as bad as elsewhere in Britain. In Stockport in 1852, Catholics clashed with anti-papists during sectarian riots, which resulted in one death and around 110 Irishmen arrested. By 1861, 5 per cent of the London population were Irish (107,000), forming the largest group of immigrants in the country.

The police, the authorities and racists alike would harass the Irish newcomers and they were often the scapegoat (and the butt of anti-Irish jokes) for much that was unequal in the country. For some British people it created a sense of superiority. However, the truth was that the majority of immigrants from Ireland were law-abiding and hard working. But due to the lack of decent housing and poor wages they often had to live cheek-by-jowl in decrepit accommodation.

**The Clerkenwell outrage**
When political moves to reinstate Irish Home Rule failed, some Irishmen attempted to escalate matters through the use of force. In 1867, two supporters of the Fenian Brotherhood were arrested while trying to buy weapons to start an uprising. After being incarcerated in Clerkenwell Prison, several of their associates attempted a daring escape plan. A barrel of gunpowder was placed by the exercise wall and ignited. It opened the prison wall and destroyed several nearby houses, killing the occupants.

A tip-off ensured the prisoners were still in their cells at the time of the detonation. Following this outrage, tensions grew in the capital, with rumours circling that the Fenians would attempt to blow up St Paul's Cathedral. In response, it is claimed that over 150,000 English people volunteered to patrol the streets of London.

**Integration** It was not just labourers who crossed the Irish Sea following the famine; many settlers were middle-class skilled craftsmen, lawyers and writers, who came in search of better wages and opportunities. Among them were those who would become influential authors, such as George Bernard Shaw, Oscar Wilde, Bram Stoker and W B Yeats. The large building contractor Murphy & Sons can trace its origins back to Ireland.

The entrepreneurial, the writers and the hard-working Irish did well in London and survived, often integrating with the British community. However, their religion was often viewed suspiciously in a predominantly Protestant country.

In the late twentieth century, however, when the 'Troubles' of Northern Ireland spilled over onto the streets of London and several bombs exploded in major UK cities, the relationship between the two communities was strained.

# EAST END

*Total walking distance 6.9km*

This walk through the East End reveals the horrific conditions that early Irish settlers had to tolerate, the founder of Chartism and a renowned social reformer.

**1 A Roman Catholic chapel destroyed** By the late eighteenth century a small contingent of Irish weavers had settled in the Spitalfields area. They had followed the Huguenot weavers, who had began arriving a century earlier. Unlike the Protestant Huguenots, the Catholic Irish had nowhere legally to practise their religion as legislation banned them from building churches. So a small, secret chapel was created for them on Ropemakers Alley (now Street). In June 1780, a large demonstration to protest the introduction of the Catholic Relief Act (CRA), and addressed by Lord George Gordon MP, got out of hand. The British were fighting wars against numerous countries at the time and needed to recruit more soldiers. Legislation had been introduced to enlist Roman Catholics into the army. However, many Protestants saw this as a dangerous move. The demonstrators included anti-Catholic Huguenot weavers and some anti-establishment factions. A petition, calling for the CRA to be repealed was handed to Parliament, but was voted down. Consequently, five days of rioting erupted across London. Much looting occurred and premises were destroyed. Catholic institutions became a target including the Bavarian Embassy and the Roman Catholic chapel on Ropemakers Alley. The situation was only quelled when 12,000 troops were deployed, resulting in 280 deaths.

**2 An Irish neighbourhood** In 1898, the social reformer Charles Booth attempted to map and gauge both the poverty and wealth of the capital in his multi-volume publication *Life and Labour of the People of London.* In his report, he refers to the inhabitants in the area around Blossom Street (**2a**) as 'Cockney Irish' (those of Irish descent, born in London), and marked the area on his map mid-blue, which the key indicated as 'Poor. 18s* to 21s* a week for a moderate family'. The exceptions were Fleur De Lis Street and Elder Street, which was occupied by middle-class Jewish people. Many of the Irish homes, two to four storeys high, were clustered around very small, dingy courtyards, often with a single water pump that supplied all the houses. Further on, in Quaker Street (**2b**), Booth reported the location as 'Rough Irish and brothels'. The area was marked as dark blue and the key read 'Very poor, casual. Chronic want'. **shillings*

**3 Battle Lines** The arrival of Irish weavers and labourers in Spitalfields during the early part of the eighteenth century caused a certain amount of tension, not only with the English-born weavers but also the newly arrived Huguenot silk weavers. Although the latter two groups were predominantly Protestant, they both had a lingering distrust of Roman Catholicism (the Huguenots had been ejected from France by a Catholic monarch). The newly arrived Irish would often accept lower wages for labouring and weaving, which resulted in clashes between the groups. In July 1736, when the old St Leonard's church was being demolished, work gangs were needed to clear the site, and a group of Irish people offered a lower price to do the work. The English workers, incensed at this undercutting, attacked the Irish. The fracas lasted for several days, with several deaths incurred. Such skirmishes over the cost of labour between English and immigrant workers would rumble on for many years.

**4 The Golden Harp** Commercial Street was carved through Shoreditch in 1857 to create a faster route from Old Street and Islington to the East End docks. Shortly afterwards, a pub, the Golden Harp, was constructed on the corner with Hanbury Street.

LEGEND
Lowest class.
Vicious, semi-criminal

It is believed it was so named to attract the growing Irish population in the area. In the mid-1930s, the pub was rebuilt and the name changed slightly, to the Golden Heart.

**5 The Dorset Street Rookeries** By the 1840s, the Spitalfields silk weaving industry established by the Huguenots had gone into decline and most of the weavers had departed *(page 13)*. The houses they vacated were by now in a poor state of repair and the rents were cheap.

It was here that many of the Irish famine victims fled, cramming as many members of their family as they could into a few rooms, and taking work as costermongers or dock labourers. A few Irish people had a trade, such as shoemaking, which they could practice from home.

For some enterprising (and often unscrupulous) people, there was an opportunity to make serious money by acquiring and renting out single rooms, often on a daily basis, to workers and their families. This type of accommodation was known as 'common lodging houses'. Jack McCarthy was a slum landlord who owned such properties in Dorset Street and elsewhere in the area. McCarthy's parents had left Ireland in 1848 and he worked initially as a bricklayer before acquiring property and several pubs. He also had controlling stakes in gambling, boxing and prostitution ventures – he was very much a Victorian 'Godfather' of the East End.

Given the dilapidated state of many houses in Spitalfields, most could be bought for very little money, and so McCarthy, with a business associate, began acquiring property in the area. They rented rooms out to male labourers who were working nearby. Single women, some divorced and with only precarious access to employment, frequently took common lodging rooms. Down on their luck, some women were forced into prostitution.

In 1888, 25-year-old Mary Jane Kelly lived in a shabby alleyway known as Miller's Court, off Dorset Street. She was born in Ireland in 1863 and had moved to London four years earlier following the death of her husband. It was in Miller's Court in late

October that Kelly met her demise. An agent of McCarthy's, who had been sent to collect the rent, found her badly mutilated body. She had become the last-known victim of Jack the Ripper. The first of the Ripper's victims, Annie Chapman, had also lived in Dorset Street. The press were now referring to the thoroughfare as 'The Worst Street in London', and at was marked on the Booth map in black.

In a twist of fate, the Jack the Ripper murders highlighted the 'depravity' and poverty of the East End and finally the government began a campaign of slum clearance. Dorset Street, later renamed Duval Street, was eventually obliterated and built over. It is now a shopping and office complex.

*Far left: a detail from Charles Booth's poverty map* (Life and Labour of the People of London, 1898). *Above: children of the slums.*

*Walking these pages 3.9km*

***1* Pearl Assurance** Patrick James Foley's parents migrated from Ireland to Leeds in the early 1830s. It was here that Foley was born, in 1836. After finishing school, Foley worked as a clerk for several mutual benefit companies before moving to London in 1857. There he established a financial self-help group named the Pearl Loan Company, which initially operated from a public house on Whitechapel Road, close to the Bell Foundry, and the first official office was just off Commercial Road. One of the main functions of the company was to enable working-class people to save money, especially to cover funeral expenses. Foley, an advocate for home rule for Ireland, was elected MP for Galway Connemara in 1885. The company grew and was renamed Pearl Assurance, with Foley as managing director. In 1914, they moved into a very grand Chancery Court building at 252 High Holborn. The company is now part of the Phoenix Group.

**2 Rally on Stepney Green** The 1848 February Revolution in France sent shockwaves across Europe, when King Louis Philippe was dethroned. Other European governments became all-too aware of rebellion and unrest in their own countries. On 29 May in the same year, 3,000 people gathered on Stepney Green to hear various speakers agitate for Irish nationalism. In Ireland and in the UK, many believed the time was right to demand home rule for Ireland. Although the British government did nothing to appease the home rule lobby, several republican movements formed, including the Fenian Brotherhood (later the Irish Republican Brotherhood) and it was one of numerous political rallies and gatherings that occurred that year.

**Feargus O'Connor & Chartism**

To qualify to vote in an British election in the nineteenth century you had to be male, aged over 21 and own property. The 1832 Reform Act had failed to extend the franchise. However, several political movements were now demanding universal male suffrage and better working conditions for all. This coalesced into a People's Charter, which was published in 1838. It demanded votes for all men over the age of 21, regardless of property owning status, plus a salary for all MPs. Chartist rallies were held across the country with many thousands in attendance.

One of the most popular orators at Chartist rallies was an Irishman, Feargus O'Connor. O'Connor was born in County Cork in 1796, to a prominent Protestant family. At the age of 18, following a fight with a group of soldiers, he fled to London to escape arrest. Here he developed a reputation for radicalism and public speaking. In 1837, O'Connor established the *Northern Star* newspaper in Leeds, which became a mouthpiece of the Chartist movement.

In 1842, a 3.3 million-signature petition calling for Chartist demands to be recognised was handed to Parliament. The government rejected the petition and a series of protest strikes followed. O'Connor was a controversial figure within the hierarchy of the Chartist movement and wasn't always liked by his fellows. In 1847, he

*Clockwise from below left: Feargus O'Connor; a plaque on Estate Road marking Dr Barnardo's first establishment; Dr Thomas Barnardo; the Ragged School Museum.*

was elected MP for Nottingham. The following year he organised the largest Chartist rally, which gathered on 10 April at Kennington Common, south London. It is believed that 150,000 people attended with plans to march on Parliament and deliver a petition containing over six million signatures. The police, fearing a huge riot, banned the march but regardless the petition was delivered, though Parliament later voted it down. Legislation was passed to prohibit further public meetings, but rallies, such as the one on Stepney Green, still went ahead a month later. The Chartist movement faded after 1848 but the radical movement splintered into smaller, diverse groups such as the UK Labour Party. Universal male suffrage would not be passed by Parliament until 1918.

***3* Dr Thomas Barnardo, philanthropist** Thomas Barnardo was born in Dublin in 1845, to a family of Jewish descent. His father had arrived from Hamburg a few years earlier. In 1866, Barnardo travelled to London to begin his medical training at the London Hospital on Whitechapel Road (**3a**), with a plan to travel on to China as a missionary. Very soon, Barnardo became aware of the horrific conditions that many children of the East End were being subjected to. He abandoned his plans to become a medical doctor (although he did adopt the title of doctor) and began to assist the homeless and destitute. His first campaign was to establish a school on Hope Place (**3b**), now Estate Road, in 1867, and to make others aware of the plight of these desperate children.

Three years later Dr Barnardo created his first children's home, on Stepney Causeway. To help raise money for his campaign he began to publish in the press 'before' and 'after' photographs of children in his care. The 'before' photos showed wretched, poorly clothed, poorly fed urchins, while the 'after' images showed the same child well dressed, healthy, and with job prospects. But as an arbitration trial would uncover some years, later many of these photographs were forged: the same child posed for both shots within a few hours of each other. It was fraud, but Dr Barnardo avoided prosecution, as photos helped to raise funds for his philanthropic work.

In 1877, with the backing of the social reformer Lord Shaftesbury, Barnardo created the first 'Ragged School', in a warehouse on the banks of the Regent's Canal (**3c**)(the building is now a museum of Victorian school life). With over 1,000 pupils, it was for some time the largest school in the capital. The pupils in attendance were fed and trained in skills useful for a working life.

Controversially, Barnardo began to despatch destitute children to Australia and Canada, sometimes against the wishes of their families. Children were effectively kidnapped and sent overseas, never to return. Regardless, Barnardo's is still a respected name today, and synonymous with the welfare of abandoned children.

# EUSTON & CAMDEN TOWN

*Total walking distance 5.8km*

Irish authors, navvies, terrorists and a pub contribute to this walk around Euston, Regent's Park and Camden.

***1* W B Yeats** William Butler Yeats became one of the major English language poets of the twentieth century. He was born in Dublin in 1865, and not long afterwards his family moved to London to enable his father to continue his art studies. Yeats' himself was educated in both London and Ireland. In 1895, the house at 5 Woburn Walk became his London base, until 1919.

Yeats' writing and poetry was inspired by the occult and spiritualism, along with Irish Nationalism. He helped to establish the Abbey Theatre, Dublin, which opened in 1904, and it became a showcase for productions portraying the 'Celtic revival' of Irish culture and literature. In the same year he established the Cuala Press, which went on to publish over 70 books, including many by Yeats himself. In 1923, he was awarded the Nobel Prize in Literature. The prize was seen by some as a symbolic accolade for Irish independence, which had been established a year earlier. In his later life, Yeats' flirted with fascism and articulated his approval of the Italian dictator Mussolini. He died in France and was buried there in 1939, although his remains were exhumed and transferred to Sligo, Ireland for reburial in 1948.

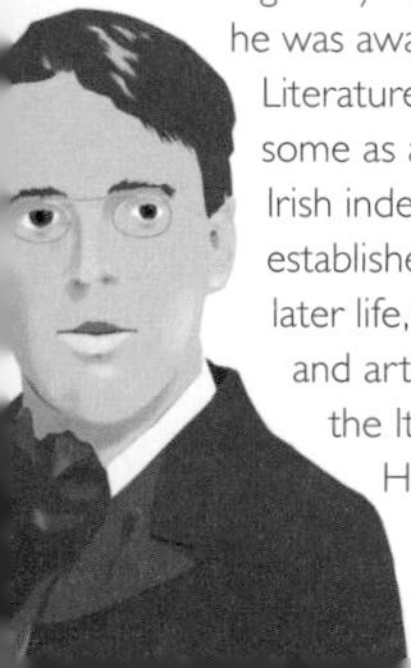

**2 George Bernard Shaw** The prolific Irish playwright and political activist George Bernard Shaw was born in Dublin in 1856. He is renowned for such works such as *Man and Superman* (1902) and *Pygmalion* (1912). Shaw was awarded the Nobel Prize in Literature in 1925 for his play *Saint Joan* and later an Oscar for his screenplay of *Pygmalion* (which became the film *My Fair Lady*, starring Audrey Hepburn).

At the age of 20, Shaw moved to London to join his mother who had fled Ireland earlier to join her lover. Following a series of minor journalistic and clerical jobs, Shaw began earning a reputation as a theatre critic. In 1882, he joined the Fabian Society and, like his friend Yeats, was an advocate of Irish Home Rule. From 1887 until 1898 he lived at 29 Fitzroy Square (Virginia Woolf would later live at the same address). His first successful play was *Arms and the Man* (1894), which, despite press criticism, gained popularity with the public and earned enough to enable him to become a full-time playwright. *Fanny's First Play* (1911), a suffragette comedy, was banned in England but played 600 times at the Abbey Theatre in Dublin. Shaw also flirted with authoritarian regimes such as Mussolini's Italy and Stalin's Soviet Russia. He died at home in Ayot St Lawrence, Hertfordshire, aged 94.

**3 IRA Bandstand bombing** A lunchtime musical performance by the 1st Battalion of the Royal Green Jackets was underway on 20 July 1982, when a bomb exploded under the bandstand. Six bandsmen were killed instantly, with one other dying a few days later. Twenty-four spectators were also injured in the attack for which the Provisional Irish Republican Army (IRA) claimed responsibility. The IRA had also struck two hours earlier in nearby Hyde Park during the Changing of the Guard ceremony, when four soldiers of the Household Cavalry were killed in a nail bomb attack. There is a memorial plaque on the restored Regent's Park bandstand. No one has ever been charged for the attack.

**4 The Dublin Castle** Camden evolved as a town in the 1820s with the arrival of the Regent's Canal. An Irish community soon began to coalesce, comprising mainly of navvies who initially dug the canals and later helped to build the railways and houses of the expanding capital. The Dublin Castle pub on Parkway became a focus for many (though not exclusively) Irish people of the area. Some of the labourers coming over from Ireland found refuge in Arlington House, just around the corner. More recently, the pub has gained a reputation as a popular music venue. Under the management of Dublin-born Alo Conlon, bands including Madness, Blur and Supergrass performed some of their early gigs here.

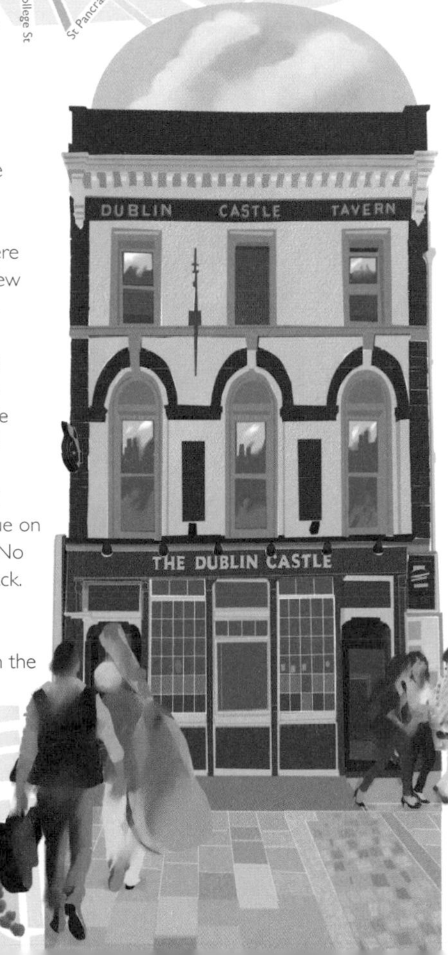

**5 The Irish Centre** The Irish Centre was established in the mid-1950s to assist many of the newly arrived Irish people seeking work and accommodation in London. Post-war, the housing on offer to recent arrivals in the major British cities could be of very poor quality, with some landlords refusing Irish immigrants accommodation altogether. The Centre was, and still is, a cultural centre, with an active programme of theatre, music and dance. On a more practical level it works to help those facing poverty and sickness. It is supported by donations from local Irish businesses and institutions.

*Clockwise from far left: William Butler Yeats; The Dublin Castle pub in Parkway, Camden; George Bernard Shaw.*

# SOUTH ASIAN LONDON

In 1599, a group of City merchants and businessmen founded the East India Company (EIC) and a year later it was granted a Royal Charter by Queen Elizabeth I to trade with countries located around the Indian Ocean (this would later expand to include South-East Asia, China and Japan).

**The First South Asians in London** Peter Pope, from south-east India, had been brought to England to train as a missionary. His anglicised name was given to him at the time of his baptism in 1616, at St Dionis Backchurch within the City. He became the first person from South Asia to undergo such a ceremony in England.

EIC trading stations were established within South Asia and managed by British staff, who employed South Asians as labourers, sailors, stock keepers and managers. Their households also employed locals as servants and ayahs (nannies). This was a far cheaper option than bringing staff from England. When the families returned home, they often brought their valued South Asian staff with them. Some ayahs were unwittingly employed just for the passage back to Britain and were then abandoned as soon as the ship docked. Although they were not great in number, this became a problem and the ayahs had to seek other employment or resort to begging. It wasn't until the late nineteenth century that a hostel was established in the East End to rescue abandoned ayahs and help them find other employment or assist with repatriation.

**Lascars** The lot of the lascar (sailors from non-European countries) was not much better. Lascars were employed on many EIC ships because, quite simply, they were much cheaper to hire than their European counterparts. However, they too could be released from employment once the ship arrived in England. Sailing ships were dependent on the weather and trade winds, so lascars could find themselves stuck in London for weeks until they could secure employment on a ship heading back to South Asia. Many resorted to begging on the streets. The EIC were eventually forced by Parliament to improve employment rights and guarantee lascars a return passage.

It is estimated that between 1850 and 1914 only several hundred South Asians were permanently resident in Britain. These were mainly chefs, servants and students who had decided to remain here.

**Students and activists** During the latter half of the nineteenth century, a small number of young South Asians arrived in London to acquire British qualifications and enhance the possibilities of working within the British-dominated administration of their homeland. Some of these students would become very influential in the South Asian independence movements. Mahatma Gandhi *(page 97)*, the 'Father of the Nation of India', studied law in London in the 1880s. Dadabhai Naoroji *(page 98)*, one of the founders of the Indian National Congress (INC), arrived in the UK and taught at London University College before becoming the first South Asian MP in Parliament. He used his platform to highlight the many injustices of British rule in South Asia.

GREATER LONDON COUNCIL
VINAYAK
DAMODAR
SAVARKAR
1883-1966
Indian Patriot
and Philosopher
lived here

**A house of sedition and revolt?** In 1905, Shyamaji Krishna Varma, an Inner Temple barrister, established India House, at 65 Cromwell Avenue, Highgate, north London. It became a hostel and first port of call for South Asian students arriving in London. India House also became a focal point for anti-colonial activists. Gandhi stayed here in 1906 and the activist and lawyer Vinayak Damodar Savarkar spoke regularly at India House meetings.

The house gained a reputation as a hotbed of sedition and revolt, with bombmaking manuals and pistols being smuggled in. Madan Lal Dhingra *(page 96)* moved here in 1908, and three years later he assassinated Sir William Curzon Wyllie. Had Dhingra been influenced by Savarkar? Scotland Yard put India House under surveillance. In 1910, Savarkar was arrested and extradited to South Asia, and India House was finally shut down.

**From ship's cook to Mayor** The number of South Asians living in London in the early twentieth century was very low. By 1932, numbers across Britain were estimated at just over 7,000. Following the First World War (in which around 1 million South Asians had been involved), some lascars decided to abandon their life on the sea and remain in Britain. A small community of Bengalis was established in Spitalfields and Whitechapel, not far from the docks. Job opportunities were available within the Jewish clothing factories and several, often former ships cooks, set up cafés for their fellow Bengalis.

After the Second World War, Britain was in need of manpower, to rebuild the damaged infrastructure, man nationalised services and work in the new National Health Service. The passing of the British Nationality Act in 1948 allowed citizens of the British colonies the right to reside in Britain. Consequently, South Asian communities grew rapidly in various parts of London, especially after India and Pakistan finally gained independence from Britain in 1947, with many people fleeing the turmoil.

A further, sudden influx of South Asians into the UK during the 1960s and 1970s led to unrest among certain sections of the British community, especially as unemployment rose during the economic downturn. Right-wing groups gathered on weekends in places such as Whitechapel, Bethnal Green and Southall to intimidate local migrant communities. Windows were smashed and fights broke out. Sadly, some members of the South Asian community were murdered, including Altab Ali *(page 91)* who had been walking home from work. These killings galvanised the second generation of South Asians into protecting themselves and campaigning for better policing and securing justice. They would not tolerate what their parents had received since arriving in London.

In 2016, Tooting born Sadiq Khan, a human rights lawyer and MP, became the first Muslim and person of Pakistani heritage to become Mayor of London.

By 2011, there were nearly one million people of South Asian descent living in London (about 12 per cent of the capital's population).

*Clockwise from far left: a group of lascar sailors on board ship; a plaque at 65 Cromwell Ave, Highgate; Mayor of London, Sadiq Khan outside City Hall; an ayah and her charge.*

# BRICK LANE

*Total walking distance 1.0km*

Brick Lane is now largely dominated by a Bengali community and is renowned for its array of South Asian restaurants. For the past 300 years the street has seen several immigrant groups arrive and move on.

**1 'Master' Ayub Ali** 'Master' Ayub Ali, a lascar from Sylhet, opened a curry café, the Shah Jolah, at 76 Commercial Street in 1920. Ali had jumped ship in the USA and then made his way to Spitalfields. He also ran a refuge for newly arrived Bengalis at nearby 13 Sandy's Row. With his good knowledge of English, Ali became an enabler for South Asian seamen in need of a bed, a job and advice. Spitalfields was then a Jewish-dominated area *(page 30)* with a large textile industry and good prospects of employment for Bengalis. As Jewish people moved out of Spitalfields to other parts of the capital, so many Bengalis moved in, buying their houses and textile businesses.

In 1943, Ali started the Indian Seaman's Welfare League, to assist mainly South Asians who were unable to return home because of the war.

**2 The Famous Clifton** One of the first curry houses designed to attract non-South Asian customers (and with a drinks licence) was The Famous Clifton restaurant at 124 Brick Lane, which opened in 1967. It had previously been a Bangladeshi café serving food to Bengali working men. The restaurant closed some years ago.

**3 Taj Stores** A Bengali seaman, Abdul Jabbar, arrived in London in 1934 and established the first Bengali grocery store in Spitalfields. Named Taj Stores, it was first established in Buxton Street before it was relocated to 112 Brick Lane, where it still trades today.

**4 Brick Lane Jamme Masjid** The Brick Lane Mosque (or Brick Lane Jamme Masjid) was established in 1976 for the local Muslim Bangladeshi community. The building has also been a place of worship for both Christian and Jewish faiths over the past few hundred years *(pages 14 & 33)*. In many ways it has come to symbolise the various migrant groups that have passed through the East End. The mosque has capacity for over 3,000 worshippers plus an education facility for local Muslim school children. The mosque attracts not only Bangladeshi Muslims but those from many parts of the world. A 30m stainless-steel minaret was added to the external structure in 2010.

**Banglatown: the Curry Capital of Europe** By 1960, it is estimated that there were 500 curry houses in Britain. Forty years later this figure had grown to approximately 8,000, and Brick Lane was once home to the largest collection of curry restaurants in Britain. The early 1980s saw the number of curry houses increase as

the district became part of the London tourist map. During the evenings, many restaurants would employ staff to entice potential customers off the street to dine in their establishment.

In 1997, the southern end of Brick Lane was branded 'Banglatown'. It was a restaurant-led initiative with decorative gateways being erected, shop facades updated and Bengali street signs added. It followed a section of Soho being named 'Chinatown' *(page 60)* for the same marketing reasons.

For some time, the scheme worked, but the influence of Shoreditch and the redevelopment of Truman's Brewery to the north, with its niche cafés, upmarket shops and street food, has eroded somewhat its gastronomic title of 'Curry Capital of Europe'.

**5 Murder of Altab Ali** During the 1970s, members of the right-wing National Front and racist skinheads would regularly gather on weekends in Whitechapel to abuse local Bangladeshi residents. Sometimes they would unleash verbal abuse, other times physical attacks on people and property. The police did little to prevent the violence . On 4 May 1978, Altab Ali, a leather garment worker, was on his way home when he was attacked by three youths on Adler Street and stabbed in the neck. He died on the spot.

Altab Ali's murder was the last straw for many South Asians who'd had enough of abuse from racist groups and violence from white, right-wing gangs. Just like the black communities *(page 78)*, they too were frustrated with being fobbed off with sub-standard accommodation and schooling. Their parents might have tolerated it, but they were not about to.

Altab Ali's funeral cortege was followed by 7,000 marchers as it detoured past 10 Downing Street. A month after Ali's murder, around 150 right-wing skinheads from various parts of London gathered to smash windows on Brick Lane.

This time they were resisted by local Bangladeshis and sent packing.

Ten years after Ali's death, the location of his murder and site of the former White Chapel church, St Mary's Park, was renamed Altab Ali Park.

In 1982, the first Bengali, Nurul Huque, was elected to Tower Hamlets council and today the borough has the largest number of South Asian and black councillors in the country. In the 2010 general election, the first Bengali, Rushanara Ali, was elected to the House of Commons.

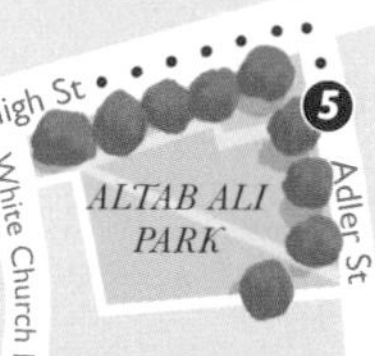


*Clockwise from far left: some of the facias and banners of Brick Lane's many curry houses; a street sign in both English and Bengali; a National Front badge from the 1970s; dancers at the Boishaki Mela (a Bengali New Year festival); the Brick Lane mosque.*

Walking these pages 1.0km

# WEST END

*Total walking distance 5.2km*

This walk through the West End reveals how South Asian cuisine has, over 250 years, been absorbed into the British palate, and how prominent South Asians have collaborated in pioneering the paperback book and the Meals on Wheels service.

## *1* The Hindoostanee Coffee House

Sake Dean Mohamed established the Hindoostanee Coffee House in 1810, at what is now 102 George Street. This 'coffee house' was in fact a South Asian restaurant and the first to be run by a South Asian *(there is a plaque in the foyer)*. Mohamed was born in Bengal in 1759 and became the first of many Bengali's to open such eateries (most South Asian restaurants in the UK today are Bengali run). Having served in the East India Company (EIC) as a surgeon, he knew that there was a market among many returning British employees (nabobs) for the food they had grown used to while serving in South Asia. Mohamed catered for this need by opening the Hindoostanee Coffee House, complete with hookahs and South Asian surroundings. Sadly, Mohamed went bankrupt within two years but he later reappeared in Brighton, opening what would become a 'royally' famous vapour baths. Earlier, in 1794, Mohamed wrote the first book to be written in English by a South Asian. It was a travel guide through parts of India.

## 3 Rabindranath Tagore

The prolific poet, musician and painter Rabindranath Tagore *(left)*, was born 1861 into a cultured and wealthy Calcutta (now Kolkata) family. Under pressure from his father, he was sent to University College London in 1878, to read law. The university was then located at Burlington Gardens (now part of the Royal Academy of Arts). However, Tagore had never fitted into the sphere of formal education and failed to get his degree. During his formative years he was often taught by his family. Tagore returned to Calcutta and continued to write verse and paint. He returned to London in 1912 and lived in Hampstead, having recently written *Gitanjali (Song*

## 2 Horatio Mohamed

Following the success of his vapour baths in Brighton, Sake Dean Mohamed decided to open a second establishment, in Ryder Street, Pall Mall, with his son Horatio managing. And like his father, Horatio was a great advocate of the benefits of bathing and often wrote on the matter. However, following the death of Mohamed senior in 1851, the business went into decline, and Horatio had to seek smaller premises in what was then Somerset Street. The new baths were located under what is now Selfridges department store.

*From far left: an Indian Hookah; the artist Rabindranath Tagore; the first publication by Pelican Book:* The Intelligent Woman's Guide to Socialism, Capitalism, Sovietism & Fascism *written by George Bernard Shaw and edited by V K Krishna Menon.*

*Offerings)*, a Bengali verse that he also translated into English. He sought W B Yeats to write an introduction to the piece. A year later, Tagore was awarded the Nobel Prize in Literature for *Gitanjali*, becoming the first non-European to receive the award. As a result, he rapidly gained international recognition.

Tagore was an outspoken supporter of Indian nationalism and opposed the rule of the British Raj in India. In 1915, he was awarded a knighthood, but he returned the honour four years later following the Amritsar massacre, when the British army fired on a large crowd of unarmed demonstrators, killing 380 people and wounding hundreds more.

Two of his musical compositions were later adopted as the Indian and Bangladeshi national anthems. There is a memorial bust of Tagore in Gordon Square *(page 97)*.

**4 Pelican Books** The polymath V K Krishna Menon had, in 1934, just become a councillor in St Pancras *(page 98)* and had also qualified as a barrister (he would later become the second most powerful man in India, after prime minister Nehru). In addition to his studies, in 1932 he began working as an editor at the publishers Bodley Head. The company was based at 8 Vigo Street and it was here that Menon met Allen Lane.

Lane had developed the concept of affordable paperback books of quality. The imprint known as Penguin Books was established in 1935. Along with Menon, Allen then co-founded Pelican Books. The first Pelican paperback to be published, in 1937, was George Bernard Shaw's *The Intelligent Woman's Guide to Socialism, Capitalism, Sovietism and Fascism*. Menon invested the money he made from Pelican Books into the India League.

**5 The Veeraswamy Restaurant** This establishment, at 99 Regent Street, is the oldest surviving Indian restaurant in the country. It was founded by Edward Palmer, a retired Indian Army officer (and great-grandson of an Indian princess), in 1926 as a meeting place not only for the Indian civil service based in London but for anyone wanting to eat South Asian food. Prior to this time, most Indian restaurants were catering only for a South Asian clientele.

**6 Norris Street Coffee House** During the eighteenth century, many officers and merchants of the East India Company had returned to Britain and retired. Large numbers were still yearning for the food they had experienced in South Asia. Sensing a gap in the culinary market, the Norris Street Coffee House in fashionable Piccadilly had begun to serve curry and rice and pilaus to its customers in 1773. This was 87 years before that other national culinary institution of fish and chips was first served up *(page 45)*. The Norris Street Coffee House also despatched curries to other parts of London. Was this possibly the first Indian take-away delivery service?

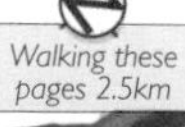

***1* Shafi's restaurant** In contrast to the Veeraswamy on Regent Street, Shafi's restaurant catered to the lower end of the market. Shafi's was established by brothers Wayseem and Rahim Mohammed, who were studying in London and had noticed a lack of good home-cooked food for fellow students. So, they opened their own restaurant at 18 Gerrard Street in the 1920s. The area then was very dilapidated, with cheap rents. With a menu of kormas, vindaloos and kebabs at affordable prices, Shafi's became a focal point for expatriates and students. Though a few Chinese restaurants had also opened in the area at the time, it was still not the Chinatown we know today.

**2 The Nanking** The anti-imperialist All-Indian Progressive Writer's Association was founded at The Nanking Chinese restaurant *(see 61)* at 4 Denmark Street in November 1934, by a group of exiled South Asian authors and poets which included Mulk Raj Anand and Sajjad Zaheer. While in London, Anand associated with and worked for V K Krishna Menon, writing propaganda articles for the independence cause. During the Second World War, Anand worked for the BBC and became acquainted with George Orwell.

**3 Meals on Wheels** Dr Harbans Lall Gulati was born in Punjab around 1896 and, following the completion of his medical training in 1919, he decided to travel to London to work as a doctor. His Indian qualifications were not recognised, so he retrained while undertaking menial work to pay for his studies.

In 1926, Gulati had requalified, and he became a general practitioner in Battersea, south London. He continued his studies at the Royal Westminster Ophthalmic Hospital on High Holborn (the hospital no longer stands) and qualified as an ophthalmic surgeon in 1945. Gulati became a Conservative councillor for Battersea in 1934. During the war, he was involved with food distribution and rationing, especially for the old and disabled, and worked closely with the Women's Volunteer Service. Post-war, Gulati expanded this Meals on Wheels service. It soon became a mobile food distribution network for people who couldn't easily prepare or access cooked meals themselves, and is still in operation today though under various names.

In 1947, Gulati switched political allegiances and joined the Labour Party, as the Conservatives would not endorse the newly proposed National Health Service.

**4 Kingsway Hall** The Kingsway Hall (**4a**)was built in 1912 as a Methodist church and became renowned as a classical music and recording venue. The Hall also saw its fair share of rallies and meetings for the cause of Indian and Pakistani independence. The British Committee of the Indian National Congress met here in 1920, to condemn the Amritsar massacre of unarmed civilians (page 93) the previous year. One speaker, the poet, suffragette and political activist Sarojini Naidu, spoke of the horrors of the slaughter.

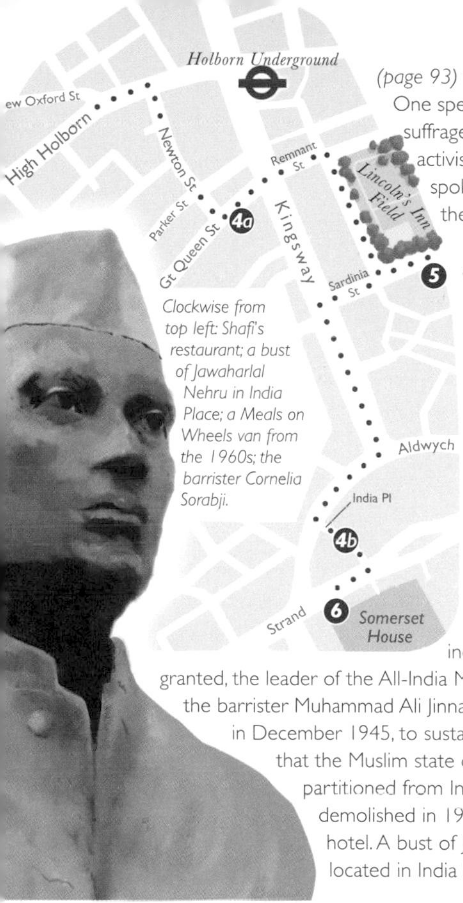

In June 1938, at a pro-Indian independence and anti-Nazi rally, the audience heard speeches from V K Krishna Menon, Jawaharlal Nehru and the black American actor, singer and political activist Paul Robeson *(page 69)*.

Several years before Indian independence was granted, the leader of the All-India Muslim League, the barrister Muhammad Ali Jinnah, spoke here in December 1945, to sustain the demand that the Muslim state of Pakistan be partitioned from India. The Hall was demolished in 1998 and is now a hotel. A bust of Jawaharlal Nehru is located in India Place (**4b**).

*Clockwise from top left: Shafi's restaurant; a bust of Jawaharlal Nehru in India Place; a Meals on Wheels van from the 1960s; the barrister Cornelia Sorabji.*

**5 Cornelia Sorabji** Cornelia Sorabji was a determined woman and was determined to break into the then all-male world of law. She was born into a Christian Parsi family in western India in 1866 and became the first female student of law at Oxford in 1889. Here she experienced much discrimination; being chaperoned to each lecture and sitting her

exams separately from the men. In 1893, she began her legal apprenticeship at Lee & Pembertons, 43 Lincoln's Inn Field, before returning to India. Despite her qualifications, the bar was closed to women until 1919. Sorabji finally became a barrister four years later.

**6 The India League** The crusade for Indian self-rule, or swaraj, had become stronger during the early twentieth century. The British government believed it had much to lose if India gained independence. A propaganda battle began to heat up. News coming out of India was censored before the British public could read it. Several Indian swaraj groups were being established in both India and Britain.

A forerunner of the India League was established in London in 1916 to lobby the British Parliament for Indian self-government and to make the British public aware of the conditions in India. In 1925, Krishna Menon had joined the League and within three years he became the joint secretary, with ambitions to make the League a more effective body. New headquarters were sited at 146 Strand and the League organised lectures, cultural events and press releases to underline the Indian perspective. The failure of the Round Table talks on independence in 1931 drove Krishna Menon to speak even more passionately at numerous rallies to highlight the inequalities of colonial rule in India and the poverty inflicted upon the India masses. By the 1940s the League had many offices across Britain.

*Walking these pages 2.7km*

# BLOOMSBURY & CLERKENWELL

*Total walking distance 3.8km*

This walk reveals many great and heroic South Asians who came to Britain and became influential politicians and doctors, plus the man who would eventually lead India towards independence.

## 1 The Bombay Emporium

Established in 1931, the Bombay Emporium, an Indian grocery store at 70 Grafton Street (renamed Grafton Way), imported direct from India and created specialist foods and spices, such as Madras curry powders, hot pickles, Pilau rice and teas. Indian students at the nearby University of London became one of their main groups of customers.

The shop was one of several such now appearing in the capital.

Raymond and Anthony Chatwell, sons of the owners, developed the business which became known as BE International. The company went on to develop several well-known household brands including Lotus and Amoy.

## 2 The Fairyland Rifle Range

This oddly named shooting range was located at 92 Tottenham Court Road (the original building no longer stands) until the outbreak of the First World War. In 1909, a Punjabi-born man, Madan Lal Dhingra, came here to familiarise himself in the handling of handguns. He was from a wealthy family and though insubordinate as a teenager, he had shown no interest in politics.

Dhingra had arrived in London, in 1906, as a student and it is known that he stayed at India House *(page 89)* in Highgate. It was here, on several occasions, that he heard the activist Savarkar speak on the subject of Indian independence and the misrule of the British Imperialists.

On 1 July 1909, Dhingra attended a meeting of the National Indian Association in South Kensington. Also present was Sir William Curzon Wyllie, an aide-de-camp to the Secretary of State for India, who was also allegedly spying on Indian student activists in London. Once there Dhingra shot and assassinated Wyllie with a handgun and was immediately arrested. Following the trial, in which Dhingra represented himself, he denounced the £100 million that Britain extracted annually from his homeland and the murder of 80 million Indians by the 'Imperial occupiers'. Seven weeks after the assassination, Dhingra was hung at Pentonville Prison in north London.

## 3 Codename 'Madeleine'

Within Gordon Square gardens there is a sculpture of the Second World War spy Noor Inayat Khan (**3a**). Khan was born in 1914 in Moscow to an American mother and an Indian father, who was a Sufi teacher. By the age of six, Khan and her family had relocated to Paris, where they would remain for the next 20 years. It was here that she became a writer and broadcaster, but after the outbreak of the Second World War and with the Germans overrunning the country, the Khan family fled to Britain.

After joining the Women's Auxiliary Air Force, Khan trained as a radio operator and, by 1943, being fluent in both French and English, she was recruited into the Special Operation Executive (SOE). Following a period of training, Khan, under the codename 'Madeleine', was flown into France to become the first undercover female radio operator to work there.

Days after her arrival in June 1943, part of her SOE group

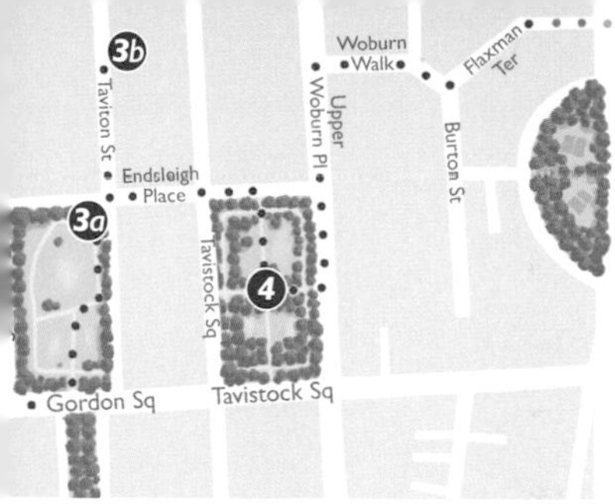


were compromised, the Gestapo making several arrests. Khan managed to avoid capture and laid low. The SOE asked her to return to London but she refused, and continued to transmit and arrange munitions drops for the French Resistance.

In October that year Khan was betrayed and captured by the Gestapo. She was interrogated and kept in solitary confinement for ten months, after which she was despatched to Dachau and executed.

Khan had volunteered to help liberate France and defeat the Nazis. She was also conscious of wanting to raise the profile of India, and had written of wanting to 'help make a bridge between the English and the Indians'. She was post-humously awarded the George Cross and French Croix de Guerre.

Prior to heading to France, Khan lived at 4 Taviton Street (**3b**). A plaque now marks the house. It is the first such commemoration of a South Asian woman.

***4* Gandhi in London** In Tavistock Square is a statue of a seated Mohandas (Mahatma) Gandhi (1869–1948). The man who informally became known as the 'Father of the Nation of India', arrived in London in 1888, aged 19, with the aim of studying law at the Inner Temple and becoming a lawyer.

By 1891, having qualified, he was called to the bar. However, in the same year he departed London and headed back to India. Unable to find work at home, he relocated to South Africa, to work as a lawyer. Here Gandhi experienced extreme abuse, at first hand, by white racists and he began a campaign against such discrimination.

During the First World War, Gandhi urged Indians living in Britain to volunteer their services in passive ways and he helped establish an Indian Field Ambulance Training Corps. There Gandhi developed the concept of *satyagraha*, a form of passive non-violent resistance and the foundation of his opposition to British imperialism in India.

In 1920, Gandhi became leader of the Indian National Congress and declared independence for India. The British government did not recognise this announcement and a summit was called. Gandhi returned to London for the Second Round Table conference in 1931. Now dressed in an Indian loincloth and shawl, he

declined the luxury of a West End hotel, opting instead to stay at Kinsley Hall, in the East End. After all, he was trying to negotiate the release of political prisoners and the removal of the salt tax. The talks collapsed and Gandhi returned to India, where he was arrested by the British rulers. While in prison he began his 'fast until death' protest, though was released once a political compromise was found.

India was finally granted independence in 1947, during which time half a million people were killed in inter-religious battles that broke out as the country was partitioned and many Muslims began migrating to Pakistan. Gandhi was assassinated in January 1948 by a Hindu extremist.

*Clockwise from left: a handbill for the Bombay Emporium; the statute of Mahatma Gandhi in Tavistock Square; Noor Inayat Khan in the uniform of the Women's Auxillary Air Force.*

*Walking these pages 1.6km*

## *1* Councillor V K Krishna Menon

Krishna Menon (1896–1976) was born into an influential Indian family and followed a career that could be described in three parts: Indian nationalist *(page 95)*, publisher *(page 93)* and British left-wing political activist. Having arrived in London in 1924 from Kerala, Menon studied at the London School of Economics and by 1937 he had concluded a law degree at the Middle Temple.

Three years earlier, Menon had become a councillor for the borough of St Pancras. He said he was as concerned for the beggars around King's Cross station as he was for the beggars of India. He spent 14 years working as a councillor in many departments, including housing, sewerage, highways and libraries. In the latter, he drastically increased the number of libraries in the borough.

During the Second World War, Menon served not only as an air raid warden but also campaigned for improved concrete shelters to be built, since the brick-built refuges were not fully bomb resistant. By the end of the war, Menon had helped found the St Pancras Arts Festival, which would later transform into the Camden Arts Festival.

In 1939 he was nominated as the prospective Labour candidate for the Dundee seat. However, the Labour Party overturned this selection, fearing Menon was a communist. This he fervently denied and suspected it was his avid Indian pro-independence stance that lost him the nomination. He resigned from the Labour Party but continued as an independent councillor. The British government were also concerned that Menon was a communist; they had his phone tapped and his mail read. Menon only stepped down as a councillor in 1947, when he became the first Indian High Commissioner in Britain.

**2 Dadabhai Naoroji MP** Born to an impoverished family in Bombay (now Mumbai) in 1825, Dadabhai Naoroji would receive, through charitable means, an excellent education, becoming a professor of mathematics and a member of the Bombay municipal council. In 1855, Naoroji moved to Britain to work as a businessman while he continued his involvement in academia, as a professor of Gujarati at University College London.

He was extremely aware of the injustices of British rule in his homeland and began lobbying Parliament, in his capacity as the president of the East India Association, for better representation. Although it was now legal for Indians to be admitted into the Indian Civil Service, the entrance exams were held in London, thus only wealthy Indians could attend. Naoroji was also acutely aware of how

HISTORIC
THE FIRST
ASIAN ELECT
TO THE HOUSE
COMMONS W
DADABHAI NA
HE REPRESENT
CENTRAL FINSB
FOR THE LIBE
PARTY FROM
1892-1895

King's Cross
St Pancras
Underground
1
Euston Road
Greys Inn Rd
Acton St
Bidborough St
Judd St
Cromer St
300m
Mabledon Pl
Flaxman Ter
Woburn Walk
Burton St

Britain was draining India economically, and yet had they no representation.

If he was to enter the British Parliament as an MP he could talk on these issues and help right many injustices. Naoroji, standing as a Liberal, won the Finsbury Central seat in 1892, by three votes, becoming the first Indian person to do so. During his campaign he had gained support from many well-known people including Keir Hardie and Florence Nightingale. While in Parliament he was assisted by Muhammad Ali Jinnah, the future founder of Pakistan. As an MP, Naoroji took up the causes of many who faced discrimination and injustice, including women's suffrage, Irish Home Rule and all matters relating to India and the inequality of British rule. The Conservative prime minister, Lord Salisbury, described Naoroji as a 'black man', and though the term was offensive, it worked to Naoroji's political advantage.

In 1895, an election was called, with the Conservatives gaining power. Naoroji lost his seat. Eleven years later, he became president of the Indian National Congress and mapped out the policy of swaraj – self-government. The following year he left Britain and returned to his native city. The 'Grand Old Man of India', as he was called, died in 1917, aged 91.

**3 The Finsbury Health Centre** Dr Chuni Lal Katial was born in the Punjab region in 1898 and, after medical training and a spell in the Indian military, he moved to Liverpool to further his career in tropical medicine. By the early 1930s he'd established a medical centre close to the Royal Victoria Dock, East London. In 1931, he arranged a meeting between Gandhi and Charlie Chaplin in the East End.

Katial later set up a medical practice in Spencer Street, Finsbury, a rundown, working-class area with inadequate medical facilities. Inspired by the former local MP and fellow Indian Naoroji, Katial stood for and became a councillor for the Finsbury Ward in 1934.

Attempts had been made to create an all-encompassing health centre in the borough before, but these had failed. Now with Dr Katial as the chair of the Public Health Committee the plans were resurrected and he commissioned the architect Berthold Lubetkin to design the new health centre. In 1938, the Finsbury Health Centre opened with a multitude of medical facilities available for locals to access, all free at the point of use. It was a forerunner of the NHS. That same year Katial was elected as the first South Asian Mayor of Finsbury.

*Clockwise from far left: V K Krishna Menon; a wall plaque to the first South Asian MP Dadabhai Naoroji on the Old Finsbury Town Hall; the Finsbury Health Centre; detail of an election poster for Dadabhai Naoroji.*

N

*Walking these pages 2.2km*

# WESTMINSTER

*Total walking distance 1.1km*

The heart of British democracy has seen many passionate South Asian politicians and campaigners, including a royal princess who became a determined suffragette, and a campaigning Labour MP.

***1* A massacre avenged** At a meeting of the East India Association at Caxton Hall, Caxton Street, on 13 March 1940, Shaheed Udham Singh stood up as Sir Michael O'Dwyer made his way to the podium to deliver a speech. Singh shot O'Dwyer twice, killing him instantly and injuring three others in the commotion.

Twenty-one years earlier, on 13 April 1919, 20,000 unarmed demonstrators assembled to protest the arrest of two pro-Indian independence leaders by the British Governor Sir Michael O'Dwyer, even though such gatherings had been banned. They were met by the British Indian Army platoon, led by General Dyer, who ordered his troops to fire directly into the crowd. Over 1,000 protestors were killed that day. Nineteen-year-old Udham Singh was in the crowd. In Britain, despite attempts to censor the massacre, there was much condemnation of the butchery.

Following the shooting of O'Dwyer, Singh was arrested and sent for trial at the Old Bailey. With Krishna Menon representing him in court, Singh used his defence to illustrate the injustices served up by the British authorities in India. However, he was hanged for murder on 31 July 1940, and buried at Pentonville Prison. Thirty-four years later his remains were returned to the Punjab region for cremation.

**2 A royal suffragette** On Friday 18 November 1910, a suffragette march of 400 women set off from Caxton Hall (**1**) to the Houses of Parliament. Led by Emmeline Pankhurst, they had hoped to meet the prime minister and discuss votes for women, but they were forcefully ejected from Parliament. Among the demonstrators was a princess.

Princess Sophia Duleep Singh was born in 1876 in London. Her father, Maharajah Duleep Singh, was a Punjabi monarch, who had been forced to abdicate at an early age by the East India Company (and would later hand over the Koh-i-Noor diamond to become part of the British Crown Jewels). Sophia, a goddaughter of Queen Victoria, grew up to become a society woman with a love of pedigree dogs, photography and cycling. Following the death of her father in 1893, she was awarded a pension of £23,000 and a grace and favour house in Hampton Court.

Duleep Singh became active in the Women's Tax Resistance League (WTRL) suffragette movement. In 1911, she was fined £3 by a Surrey Court for having an unlicensed coach and dogs. She refused to pay the fine and later a bailiff seized some of her jewellery, which was then auctioned off. However, it was bought by a member of the WTRL and returned to Duleep Singh. This action was repeated many times over.

In the same year, Duleep Singh threw herself in front of Prime Minister Asquith's car in Downing Street while protesting for women's votes. Upon the outbreak of war the suffragette movement ceased its campaign and Duleep Singh became a nurse, treating soldiers injured in battle. Finally, in 1928, women over the age of 21 were granted the vote. The name and image of Duleep Singh appears on the statue of suffragette Millicent Fawcett in Parliament Square.

**3 Shapurji Saklatvala MP** The anti-imperialist Shapurji Saklatvala was a brilliant orator who became a champion of Indian independence, Irish Home Rule and of workers' rights both in India and Britain. He was born in Gujarat in 1874, into a wealthy family with connections to the Tata industrial empire. During the bubonic plague that struck Bombay in the late nineteenth century, Saklatvala assisted those most afflicted. In 1905, he briefly moved to Manchester to manage Tata's office, but he soon departed to study law in London and become a barrister.

Once in Britain, Saklatvala's communist beliefs deepened. He joined the Independent Labour Party and spoke at many rallies in support of oppressed groups, and marched with the suffragettes. In 1922, he stood as a Labour candidate in the working-class area of North Battersea and won the seat. Though he lost it the following year, he was re-elected in 1924, this time as a communist candidate as he felt the Labour Party was not radical enough. In Parliament he spoke of the chronic exploitation of the Bengali jute workers by British industrialists.

During the General Strike of 1926, Saklatvala was arrested for sedition and imprisoned for two months. A year later, during a visit to India, he spoke at many rallies, met Gandhi and Nehru, and was lauded as a hero. As a consequence of his campaigning he was put under surveillance by British intelligence.

He lost his Commons seat in 1929 and then attempted several comebacks but to no avail; in the St Pancras constituency, he was defeated by the Labour candidate Krishna Menon *(page 98)*. Saklatvala continued to tour and agitate in the name of communism until his death in 1936.

**4 The Commons and Lords**
In 1892, Dadabhai Naoroji *(page 98)* became the first London MP of South Asian birth to enter Parliament. When Saklatvala (**3**) was voted out in 1929, it would be nearly 60 years before Keith Vaz became MP for Leicester East. And it wasn't until 2010 that Rushanara Ali became the first Bangladeshi-born MP, for the constituency of Bethnal Green. She was also one of the first female Muslims MPs to enter the Commons. Sadiq Khan became a Labour MP for Tooting in 2005 but resigned his seat in 2016 becoming the first Mayor of London born to South Asian parents.

Working in his capacity of Under-Secretary of State for India, the lawyer Satyendra Prasanna Sinha was awarded a hereditary peerage and became Baron Sinha of Raipur in 1919, so becoming the first South Asian person to sit in the House of Lords.

*Clockwise from far left: Shaheed Udham Singh; Princess Sophia Duleep Singh selling copies of* The Suffragette*; Shapurji Saklatvala MP; a newspaper cutting reporting Duleep Singh's court appearance for unpaid taxes; statue of Mahatma Gandhi* (page 97) *in Parliament Square.*

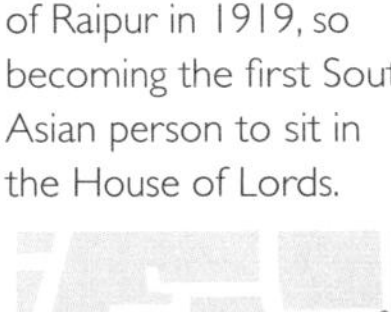


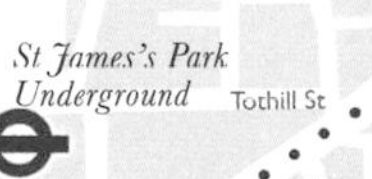

Westminster Underground
Parliament St
Bridge St
St James's Park Underground
Tothill St
Broadway
Caxton St
Victoria Street
Gt Smith St
Abingdon St
Millbank
RIVER THAMES

Walking these pages 1.1km

CRIMINAL COURTS

PRINCESS'S UNPAID TAXES.

FINES UPON FOUR SUMMONSES.

The Princess Sophia Duleep Singh, residing at Hampton-road, Hampton Court, attended at Feltham Police Court yesterday upon summonses for refusing to pay taxes. She employed a groom without a licence, and also kept two dogs and a carriage without paying for the necessary licences.

# SOUTHALL

***Total walking distance 2.9km***

Southall is a town 17km to the west of London. Since the 1950s, it has grown into the largest Punjabi community outside South Asia.

Following the partition of India in 1947, the state of Punjab was split between the newly formed Muslim state of Pakistan and India. Great upheaval resulted, as people moved in their thousands across the border, fearing reprisals from religious and political opponents. Some, including many male Sikhs, migrated to Britain and especially to Southall.

Post-war companies in Southall were desperate for employees, especially in the areas of clothing, food and metal production.

The men (and it was just men – their wives would follow during the 1960s) would live several to a room, in small terraced houses. Many early arrivals occupied houses on Hambrough and Abbots Road, just off the Broadway. To service the requirements of the new arrivals, some Punjabis established small 'corner' shops. To cater for factory shift workers, they would open early and close late ('open all hours').

By 1982, over 70 per cent of Southall residents were of South Asian or British South Asian origin, the Sikh community forming the largest group, and Southall earned the nickname 'Little India'. It is London's most South Asian neighbourhood, with an equally large South Asian shopping area.

***1* R Woolf & Co Rubber Factory** One company that was very keen to employ Punjabis was the rubber factory of R Woolf & Co. One of the company's managers had served in the war with Punjabi soldiers and he advertised in Punjab state encouraging men to migrate to Southall to work in the factory, which supplied rubber components for the motor industry among others. By 1967, 97 per cent of its unskilled factory staff were Punjabi Sikhs and they often received lower pay than their white counterparts. The Art Deco factory stood on Uxbridge Road but was eventually demolished to make way for the Bridge Retail Park.

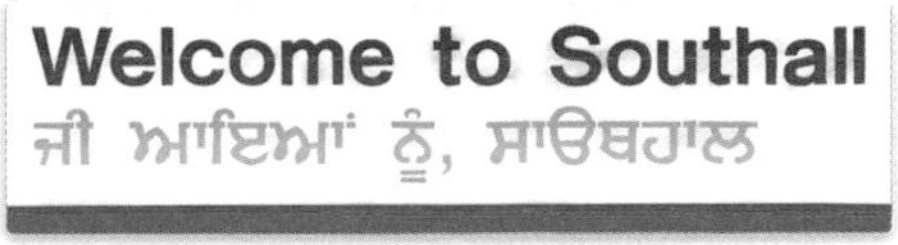

**2 The Hambrough Tavern** On the evening of Friday 3 July 1981, several hundred skinheads were bussed in to hear the band The Four Skins play at the Hambrough Tavern. When they arrived some of them smashed shop windows, damaged cars and gave Nazi salutes.

Word of the events quickly spread throughout Southall. The Southall Youth Movement (SYM) and local South Asians gathered on the Broadway to protest at the sudden appearance of fascists and to protect their neighbourhood. The two groups launched bricks at each other with the police now positioned in the middle and on the receiving end of many projectiles. The riot continued for over four hours and the Tavern was partially burnt down. Later, the local South Asian community accused the police of not protecting them from the fascists.

**3 Blair Peach** On St George's Day, 23 April 1979, in the run-up to the general election, the National Front held a rally at Southall Town Hall (**3a**) for their local candidate, with activists being bussed in from other parts of London. Despite opposition to the event from many quarters, including the SYM, the meeting went ahead. The assembly was seen as being provocative in such a well-known immigrant area. 4,000 police were drafted in to protect those few hundred attending the meeting. The demonstrators threw bricks and bottles at the police and those attending the rally. Mounted officers then charged to disperse the attackers.

Attending the demonstration was a New Zealander and Anti-Nazi League member,

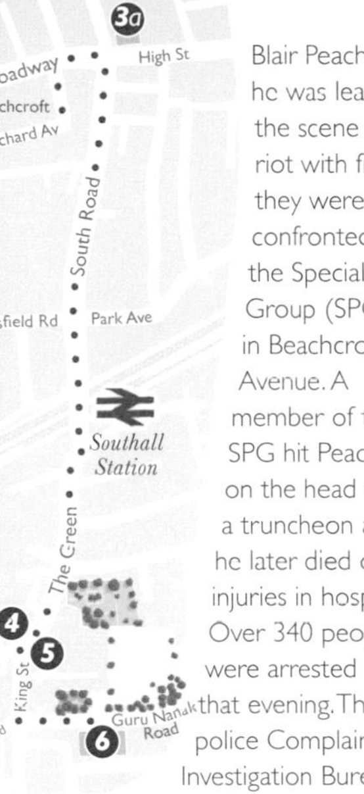


Blair Peach. As he was leaving the scene of the riot with friends, they were confronted by the Special Patrol Group (SPG) in Beachcroft Avenue. A member of the SPG hit Peach on the head with a truncheon and he later died of his injuries in hospital. Over 340 people were arrested that evening. The police Complaints Investigation Bureau report into the death of Blair Peach was eventually published in 2009, 30 years later. No police officer was ever identified nor charged with his 'murder'.

**4 Indian Workers Association (Southall)** The IWA (Southall) is a union that was established in 1956 to protect immigrant workers' rights on pay, conditions and injustices. Many of its early members could not read or write English and some traditional British unions didn't understand the needs of the new immigrants. Despite popularity among Punjabi workers, by the mid-1960s working conditions at R Woolf & Co became a serious issue.

In 1965, the IWA became heavily involved in leading workers out on strike following the suspension of a South Asian employee for poor timekeeping. The company responded with a lockout and attempted to recruit new South Asian staff from Bradford, West Yorkshire. However, this plan failed, and six weeks later the owners conceded to the demands.

**5 Gurdip Singh Chaggar** An 18-year-old student, Gurdip Singh Chaggar, was stabbed to death in a racist attack, involving several white teenagers on 4 June 1976 outside the Victory pub (the building no longer stands). Within days, the Southall Youth Movement (SYM) was formed. Under the banner 'Here to Stay, Here to Fight', the SYM, composed of mainly second-generation South Asians, stated that it would no longer tolerate racial attacks and abuse. The formation of the SYM was a key moment in the battle against racism in Britain. In the following years similar groups would fight back when attacked *(page 91)*.

The police played down the racial provocation for the murder, and the judge at the trial of the two accused teenagers also claimed that there were no racist intentions in the attack. The defendants were found guilty of manslaughter and sentenced to four years each in prison. In 1976, in the eyes of the authorities, racism simply didn't exist in Britain.

**6 Gurdwara Sri Guru Singh Sabha**

A gurdwara is a place of worship and assembly for Sikhs. In 1964, the first gurdwara in London was established at a terraced house in Beaconsfield Road. However, as the Sikh population of Southall grew, so the need for a larger building arose.

The Sri Guru Singh Sabha Southall is now part of the largest gurdwara organisation outside India. The Sikh temple was inaugurated in 2003 and the main hall can accommodate a congregation of up to 3,000 worshippers. The langar, or free kitchen, can serve up to 20,000 vegetarian meals a week.

*Clockwise from far left: a railway station sign in English and Gurmukhi; 18-year-old Gurdip Singh Chaggar; the Gurdwara Sri Guru Singh Sabha; an Anti-Nazi League banner following the death of Blair Peach.*

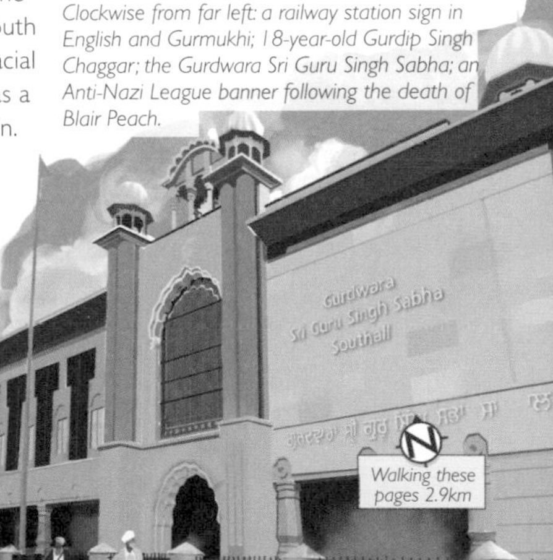

# ACKNOWLEDGEMENTS

My thanks to all who have assisted me in creating this book. These include: Katherine Cheng, Andy Merriman and Jeffrey Green, for bringing to my attention a monograph on the life of Dr Philip Lamb (born Ping Win Lam), written by his daughter, Jane Farmar ☙ The guide and author Rachel Kolsky ☙ Barry Musikant for allowing me access to the Old Velho Cemetery ☙ Arthur Torrington of the Equiano Society ☙ Miriam Keaveny of the Wellcome Collection ☙ Also my appreciation to: Stephen Cooper, Florence Fathers, Tony Foo, John Halligan, Kevin Harrison, Christine Malik, Maleiha Malik, Ian Shacklock and Marion Vargaftig.

Thanks also go to Elizabeth Multon, Jenny Clark and Kathryn Beer at Bloomsbury for assisting me with the production of *Diverse London* and for allowing me the freedom to write, illustrate and design this book as I had originally envisaged.

And finally, a huge thanks to my wife, Sheila Fathers, for her assistance in the creation of this book and for walking many of the routes with me.

# SELECTED BIBLIOGRAPHY


Ackroyd, Peter, *London, The Biography*, Chatto & Windus 2000

Black, Dr Gerry, *Jewish London, an Illustrated History*, Breedon Books 2003

Bradley, Simon & Pevsner, Nikolaus *The Buildings of England*, Yale University Press 2005

Burke, Thomas, *Limehouse Nights*, Books of Library Press 1969

Chatterjee, Arup K, *Indians in London*, Bloomsbury 2021

Coogan, Tim Pat, *Wherever Green Is Worn*, Random House 2000

Cruickshank, Dan, *Spitalfields. The History of a Nation in a Handful of Streets*, Windmill 2016

Fathers, David, *Bloody London*, Conway/Bloomsbury 2020

Fishman, William J, *The Streets of East London* Five Leaves 2015

Fryer, Peter, *Staying Power: The History of Black People in Britain*, Pluto Press 2018

Gwynn, Robin D, *The Huguenots in London*, The Alpha Press 1988

Gwynn, Robin D, *Huguenot Heritage*, Routledge & Kegan Paul 1985

Hollen Lees, Lynn, *Exiles of Erin: Irish Migrants in Victorian London*, Cornell University Press 1979

Janvrin, Isabelle & Rawlinson, Catherine, *The French in London*, Wilmington Square Books 2013

Kolsky, Rachel & Rawson, Roslyn, *Jewish London*, New Holland 2012

Leventhal, Michael & Goldstein, Richard, *Jews in Britain* Shire 2013

Lichtenstein, Rachel, *On Brick Lane*, Penguin 2008

Lichtenstein, Rachel & Sinclair, Iain, *Rodinsky's Room*, Granta 2000

London, Jack, *People of the Abyss*, Seawolf Press 2017

Phillips, Mike & Phillips, Trevor, *Windrush*, Harper Collins 1998

Price, Barclay, *The Chinese in Britain: A History of Visitors and Settlers*, Amberley 2019

Rocker, Fermin, *The East End Years: A Stepney Childhood*, Freedom Press 1998

Sardar, Ziauddin, *Balti Britain: A Provocative Journey Through Asian Britain*, Granta 2009

Visram, Rozina, *Asians in Britain, 400 Years of History*, Pluto Press 2002

Winder, Robert, *Bloody Foreigners: The Story of Immigration to Britain*, Abacus 2013

Yee, Chiang, *The Silent Traveller in London*, Interlink Books 2002

Zangwill, Israel, *Children of the Ghetto: A Study of a Peculiar People*, Grierson Press 2016


# SELECTED WEBSITES

**General websites**

banglastories.org
beyondbanglatown.org.uk
huguenotsociety.org.uk
nurturingthenation.org.uk
ourmigrationstory.org.uk
spitalfieldslife.com

**Online archives**

britishnewspaperarchive.co.uk
newspapers.com

**Web-based maps**

google.co.uk/maps
layersoflondon.org
openstreetmap.org

# PICTURE CREDITS

Page 18 *A detail of the London map surveyed by John Rocque* (1746).

Page 31 *Merry-Go-Round*, 1916, Mark Gertler. Purchased 1984. © Tate, Photo: Tate.

Page 76 *Richard and Maria Cosway, and Ottobah Cugoano*. An etching by Richard Conway (1784). Yale Centre for British Art, Paul Mellon Collection.

# GLOSSARY

**Banglatown:** An area of restaurants and shops around the southern end of Brick Lane and Osborn Street. The name came into existence in the late 1990s.
**Bombay:** A large Indian city, renamed as Mumbai in 1995.
**Calcutta:** An Indian city, renamed as Kolkata in 2001.
**Chinatown:** The first Chinatown came into existence in the late nineteenth century in London's East End district of Limehouse. Following the Second World War, several Chinese restauranteurs moved their establishments to Soho in central London, where at the time the rents were cheap. By the 1980s, the area around Gerrard Street had become known as Chinatown.
**Lascar:** From the seventeenth century a lascar was an Indian sailor who worked on ships belonging to the East India Company. Later the name lascar was applied to nearly all non-European sailors.
**Londinium:** The Roman name for the City of London.
**South Asia:** A geographic area that encompasses the countries of Afghanistan, Bangladesh, Bhutan, India, Nepal, Pakistan and Sri Lanka.

# INDEX

CONWAY
Bloomsbury Publishing Plc
50 Bedford Square, London, WC1B 3DP, UK



First published 2022



A catalogue record for this book is available from the British Library

ISBN: 978-1-8448-6556-7; ePub: 978-1-8448-6555-0; ePDF: 978-1-8448-6554-3

2 4 6 8 10 9 7 5 3 1

Typeset in 8 on 10.2pt Gill Sans Light by David Fathers
Printed and bound in India by Replika Press Pvt. Ltd.

To find out more about our authors and books visit www.bloomsbury.com and sign up for our newsletters

**Note:** While every effort has been made to ensure the accuracy of this guidebook, changes can occur over time. If you discover any important changes to the routes in this book, we're happy to hear about them. Please email us at adlardcoles@bloomsbury.com with any comments.